House Calls with John

by

John Radebaugh M.D.

PETER E. RANDALL PUBLISHER LLC
Portsmouth, New Hampshire 03802
2006

Second printing 2007

ISBN: 1-931807-46-9

Library of Congress Control Number: 2005911056

Published by:

Peter E. Randall Publisher LLC
Portsmouth, New Hampshire 03802
www.perpublisher.com

Book design: Grace Peirce

Additional copies of this title may be obtained from:
John F. Radebaugh
6 Blueberry Lane C49
Falmouth, Maine 04105

Foreword

*G*reetings colleagues. As primary care physicians, you are leaders in the future of patient care. You are a caring, dedicated group of physicians, adaptable to a variety of conditions, always interested in the welfare of your patients and their families. As a family practitioner who has practiced in many areas of the country, I have walked in your shoes.

Most of you are overworked, inundated with a variety of insurance demands, concerned with dwindling reimbursements, and doing your best to navigate the available community resources to improve your patients' lives. As your patients age, they will require more rehabilitative services, additional specialists, and numerous community resources. To best address the complex care needs of your patients, medical house calls can help improve patient care and, in turn, help you rediscover why you chose the medical profession in the first place.

Although you may appreciate the increasing need for house calls, you may find it hard to fathom how you will be adequately compensated for this type of care delivery. Many of you have debts from medical school and training while the cost of educating your own children is skyrocketing. As malpractice insurance rates continue to climb—especially for those of you with obstetrical responsibilities—it is imperative that we explore new solutions that enhance the quality of patient care and the quality of our own lives.

There is a brighter future for you and your patients and we as a profession may help to bring this about. With this in mind, may you find this book to be an inspirational read.

Warmly,

John Radebaugh, M.D.

Contents

John Radebaugh M.D.

Introduction

I have known John Radebaugh as teacher, mentor, colleague, and friend for the past thirty-six years. I first met him in the fall of 1969, during my first year at the University of Rochester School of Medicine, where he was a faculty member in the Department of Pediatrics. In my Preventive Medicine course that fall, taught by Naomi Chamberlain, another remarkable member of the medical school's faculty in those years, I learned about the many migrant farm worker camps just west of Rochester, New York. Through Naomi's wise teaching of the ways that social and environmental conditions influence people's health, I became interested in learning much more about the factors affecting the health of the local farm workers.

A few years earlier, Dr. Radebaugh, inspired by Naomi Chamberlain and supported by Dr. Robert Berg, chair of the Department of Community Medicine at Rochester, and Dr. Robert Haggerty, the chair of the Department of Pediatrics, had started a migrant health program. As a first-year medical student, I had the opportunity to volunteer at a health clinic at one of the outlying farms. Also, I joined John for some of the many house calls that form a foundation for his story, *House Calls with John*. I saw horrible living conditions, contaminated water supplies, and inadequate toilet facilities. I met families who, in spite of such conditions and other severe stress, demonstrated extraordinary resiliency. I saw Dr. Radebaugh in action, his dignity and respect for the patients, the precision and care with which he diagnosed complex cases, the bright sparkle in his eyes, the signature harmonica that he carried with him, and his tireless determination to address the injustices that were frequently the root causes of the illness at hand.

In the summer of 1970, between my first and second years of medical school, I joined John at the Clinica de Salubridad de Campesinos in Brawley, California, where he helped to organize a health care system in which farm workers themselves had a significant voice from the start. In September 1975, during my pediatric residency at Rochester, I spent a month with John at a clinic near Fresno, California, administered by the United Farm Workers Union under Cesar Chavez, who was a huge inspiration for John. I then had only occasional contact until 1986, when our paths intersected again. He had just joined a primary care preceptor program for medical students at Dartmouth Medical School. By then, I had moved into a public health career in maternal and child health with the state of Vermont. Most recently, in 2002, we ended up in close proximity in Maine, as I became the director of Maternal and Child Health with the state of Maine.

As it is with people who approach life and live according to their conscience and sense of justice, John encountered obstacles and controversies just about everywhere he went. I witnessed such tensions in Rochester and California, where John's passion to serve the poor and oppressed clashed with entrenched systems that fell shamefully short in honoring our common and interconnected humanity. In addition, he profoundly respected the unique culture of our diverse communities. His deep concern for historically marginalized and exploited populations challenged people of privilege and wealth to address the great moral issues confronting our society. Somehow, through these storms, many of which are described in this book, John managed to sustain his own dignity. His career as a physician expeditionary and risk taker reminds us that the courage to live up to the highest ideals of the medical profession will inevitably generate controversy.

It is an understatement to say that John Radebaugh inspired me, as he has done for many people over the past fifty years, the patients for whom he cared, the students for whom he left a lifelong impression. and the colleagues for whom he modeled the highest qualities of a precise and always learning clinician who integrated social activism into his practices. In *House Calls with John*, combining his wit and humor and profound insight into the essence of medical practice, he rekindles the spirit that inspired many of us to aim for the making of compassion, service, advocacy, and the quest for peace and justice at the heart of our medical profession.

At a time of unconscionable health inequalities, a growing gap between the rich and the poor, and a chaotic health care system that is more preoccupied with managed rather than humane care, Dr. Radebaugh's story, as told here, is of urgent importance.

Richard A. Aronson, M.D., M.P.H.
Medical Director, Maternal and Child Health
Department of Health and Human Services, Augusta, Maine

Preparation Years

*T*his narrative is a series of highlights of my peripatetic career in medicine in many parts of the United States. Many of the events involve migrant farm workers, on both the East Coast and the West Coast, some with community health programs, one with Cesar Chavez as a volunteer. As my career unfolded, I was increasingly involved with house calls, hence the title. I learned the value of a home visit in an attempt to understand a patient or family in much more depth than is possible in the usual office visit. The hustle and bustle of the usual medical practice allows only a superficial knowledge of the patient as a person. Sometimes that unknown person is central to the success of therapy, which, in most instances, is more than just the medicines prescribed. In addition, I learned much from patients, who taught me to listen, and to take time to hear their stories, and in so doing, I gained a deep respect for them as individuals.

"The philosophy of patient care is in caring for the patient." This is a much quoted maxim by Francis W. Peabody, M.D., as described in the *Journal of the American Medical Association* (vol. 88, #12, pp. 813–818 March 19, 1927). This made an indelible imprint on my practice of medicine, as I will illustrate later.

First, I want to give you an idea of my personal background. I was the oldest of three children in Greenfield, Massachusetts. The Depression of 1929–30 affected our family significantly. My father lost his job as a fuel oil salesman, and my mother, as a kindergarten teacher, was unable to support our family on her modest salary. My grandfather, a Congregational minister, whose wife died a few years previously, invited us to live in his home in Springfield, Massachusetts. He was a model of humbleness and selflessness, of dedication to service for his parishioners. I wrote a short biography about him, entitled "A Shepherd to His Flock," while I was in high school. I also worked as an orderly in one of the local hospitals, where I was allowed to observe an orthopedic surgeon perform a knee operation: *"Yes, I want to do that some day,"* I thought to myself.

I was allowed to defer the draft for six months until high school graduation in June 1943, then spent a rotation in the infantry, in the Army Special Training Program at Pasadena Junior College, California, in a tank training program in Texas, and finally in the paratrooper training program at Fort Benning, Georgia. I suffered a broken arm, then was transferred to the West Coast as an infantry replacement to become part of an invasion of the Japanese mainland. On August 6, 1945, the first atomic bomb destroyed Hiroshima, and soon the second accomplished similar devastation to Nagasaki. Later, I visited some of the Japanese defenses as an occupation troop, and realized that my survival on those beachheads was highly unlikely.

During my six months in Japan, I developed a great respect for the people and their respect for the environment. I became close to a Japanese Methodist minister and his family, and later sent the Japanese edition of the *Reader's Digest* to their teenage son for five years. While in Japan, I was able to transfer to the medical corps, where I was taught a number of laboratory skills by a young physician, one other stimulus for my medical ambitions. Before leaving Japan, I had an opportunity to rejoin the paratroopers to complete jump training. I was discharged from the Army on February 15, 1946, and, much to my surprise, met my younger brother Dave, who started his Army career by passing out clothing to recently discharged veterans, including me. I was anxious to be accepted into a college for the spring term, and was admitted to Bates College because another applicant dropped out of the admission process. The GI Bill was a superb benefit, and supplied most of my monetary needs at Bates and later at medical school.

Bates, as a liberal arts institution, offered a balanced curriculum of sciences and humanities, to which I added a summer semester at Bowdoin and another at the University of New Hampshire. This allowed me to finish college in two and a half years. A number of professors were major mentors for me, including Dr. Andres Myhrman, in sociology; Dr. Rayborn Zerby in cultural heritage, a two-year course regarding significant cultural events of Western history; Dr. William Sawyer, in biology; and Dr. Fred C. Mabee, in chemistry. A Phi Beta Kappa and Bates College Club graduate, I relished the academic environment, but was unable to participate in many of the extracurricular activities, a true personal loss.

A personal gain was the result of my courtship with Dorothy Paine, whom I knew in high school and to whom I was engaged for a year before our marriage on June 7, 1947, at a tiny church in North Sebago, Maine. Our wedding was an electrifying experience, for lightning struck the church steeple the night before the ceremony. My grandfather, the minister, and Rev. Albert C. Niles, another relative and a Universalist minister, combined their skills to make certain that this was a doubly binding union, the truth of which has been evident in succeeding years.

Accepted at Harvard Medical School, I felt a bit overwhelmed by the amount of hours needed to complete the assigned studies. The faculty was impressive, the buildings imposing, and I was uncertain of my first-year survival. I worked as a scrub nurse in one of the hospitals and Dotty worked as a secretary in the Harvard Gift Office to help our budget. Later, I became a weekend bacteriologist at Children's Hospital, and as a blood bank technician at Massachusetts General Hospital.

Having survived the freshman year, I found the next three years much more to my liking, for pathology, which became one of my favorite courses, provided an understanding of disease processes from the cellular level. We also had an opportunity to examine patients for the first time, a brief introduction to the living patients that most of us would be seeing for the rest of our careers. During one of my first days on the hospital wards, I examined an older woman whom I suspected of heart failure. "What did you think of her extremities?" my preceptor inquired. "I didn't notice anything unusual," I responded. "She is completely paralyzed on her left side," he commented.

A few days later Dr. William Castle, a Nobel Prize nominee, asked me about my findings in an older male who was an alcoholic. "I think that he has breath sounds indicating some type of lung problem," I volunteered. "Those were normal breath sounds; now listen to his heart with me," he said. The patient was in high output heart failure, due in part to thiamine deficiency related to his alcoholism.

These two examples were one of the best ways to learn by mistakes, especially while under expert supervisors. Imagine how fortunate I felt with a Nobel Prize nominee as my preceptor. During the next three years, we were immersed in a variety of clinical experiences in five different hospitals. I worked with Dr. Leonard Kurland in a survey of patients with multiple sclerosis, and as a result, he offered me an internship in neurology at the Mayo Clinic. I was excited at the offer, but was counseled to take a more general internship by my adviser, a fine surgeon, who said, "A wide background will offer you an opportunity to learn whether you really want to be a neurologist, at which time you can make a more educated choice."

With that advice, I applied for a rotating internship at Mary Hitchcock Memorial Hospital in Hanover, New Hampshire, which Dotty and I felt gave us a change from city living and a better environment for our two young children, George, age three, and Alan, age one. Not owning a car, we walked everywhere in Hanover, and for a real treat ate Sunday dinners at the hospital cafeteria. Living in portable housing, heated by kerosene, and covering our windows with plastic during the winter, we were fortunate not to succumb to carbon monoxide poisoning, probably saved by the uninsulated walls of our cottage.

During one of my monthly rotations, I admitted an elderly woman scheduled for surgery on the next day to remove a growth from the back of her throat. From her history, I learned that she noted afternoon weakness in her eyes and difficulty in swallowing every afternoon. Suspecting myasthenia gravis, an immune condition involving nerve conduction, I gave her a small injection of neostigmine methyl sulfate, a treatment for this condition. Immediately her eyes opened wide, swallowing improved, and the mass in the back of her throat disappeared. The mass was related to the relaxing of her swallowing muscles with her malady. I had seen several similar problems while a medical student. She avoided surgery, and her surgeon made certain that I examined the patient during each of her return visits.

The rotating nature of my internship allowed me to pick from a number of clinical avenues for the next phase of my career. After a stimulating rotation in pediatrics, I applied and was accepted at Massachusetts General Hospital for further training in pediatrics. Thoughts of a career in neurology faded from my plans, probably a too specialized field for my more general interests.

At Massachusetts General Hospital, chaired by Dr. Allan Butler, a fine teacher and an outspoken advocate for patients' rights and universal health care, I came under the influence of Dr. Frederic M. Blodgett, who made many house calls in the westend of Boston. This was an area of tenement housing in a neighborhood he knew well. I accompanied him on some of these calls, where many of his clients called down from their apartments, "Hello, Dr. Blodgett," and he usually replied with their names. On one occasion, I was especially impressed when he arrived at the apartment of a sick child in a fourth-floor flat. Outside the apartment was in poor condition, but inside it was kept immaculate. Here, he was at his best as he listened to the mother describing the illness. He put her and the child at ease, and examined while he explained exactly what he was doing. He obtained a throat culture of the patient, who had tonsillitis, and left some medicine while reassuring the mother that he would return in two days to check on her child's progress.

This was one of my earliest experiences with house calls. I immediately realized the importance of such calls for families without transportation or with few resources. I also appreciated the dignity with which Dr. Blodgett approached patients, and their confidence in his caring manner.

The pediatric residency was a fine clinical experience for a general pediatrician, but also exposed the resident to the finest of specialists when needed. For example, we were introduced to a patient from Pawtucket, Rhode Island, with an unusual disease. He was thought to have diabetes mellitus, but on examination we found no sugar in the urine and a normal blood glucose. His breathing and severe dehydration suggested that he was in diabetic acidosis. What was the matter with this child? Fortunately, a pediatric research assistant suggested that we look for cystine crystals in the cornea of his eyes, which were located by an ophthalmologist at the Massachusetts Eye and Ear Infirmary next door to the pediatric department. A slit lamp examination revealed these crystals, and X-ray crystallography identified them specifically. Another resident and I spent much of the night studying the details of this illness, and the next morning presented this child with cystine storage disease to the rest of the staff, all within twenty-four hours of his admission. Further history revealed that there were several other relatives who had a similar wasting illness. I was allowed to visit the physician in Pawtucket to explain our findings, though we were unable to offer a treatment to cure this inherited malady.

Occasionally grateful families want to show appreciation for the care shown to their child. Once I was given a frozen codfish wrapped in a newspaper. It was a hot summer afternoon and I carried it to the nearest subway stop. Soon the newspaper was soaked from the melting ice, as was I. Worse than that, the associated fishy odor caused passengers at my section of the subway to seek distant seats until I was the lone inhabitant of my section of the subway car. I never tasted the contents of that gift, for by the time I reached home it was not fit to eat.

Our family increased by one with the arrival of our third child, Susan, who provided a lusty addition to our family. She also signaled the need to finish my training and start to earn a living for Dotty and our three children. In addition, we bought our first car, at our age of thirty-one years. It was a ten-year-old Pontiac in good condition, built like a tank, offering safe transportation for our family.

Bangor, Maine

After looking at several places, we settled in Bangor, Maine, where I bought a small home, and, in keeping with other physicians in that city, planned to have a small home office. In August 1955, I placed a sign, PEDI-ATRICS, and awaited patients. My first was a woman who brought her dog! This was not an auspicious start for a medical practice.

After one week of no patients, and with no income, and with mounting bills, I had to make a decision for funds. It was the beginning of the potato - picking season in Aroostock County, one hundred miles to the north, and I rented a small room in Houlton, Maine. I picked potatoes for four days until it started to rain steadily. What little money I earned was disappearing rapidly until a phone call to Dotty revealed that someone had made an appointment. Back home, happily, I stepped into the waiting room to greet my first patient, only to find that our new puppy had left his calling card in the middle of the waiting room. Embarrassed, I cleaned up the rug and then invited in the mother and child for an interview and examination.

Other patients soon followed, but initially only in dribbles. I had created a small laboratory in a former pantry next to the examining room. I was able to perform blood counts, including hemoglobins, and throat cultures, which I incubated in a small cardboard box heated with a fifteen-watt bulb, which provided the proper temperature, 98.6 degrees. I attained the proper temperature by using a thermometer to measure the temperature created by different-sized lightbulbs, and the fifteen-watt bulb was a perfect source of heat.

Each morning I reviewed the cultures with the hospital bacteriologist, who was most helpful to me. She provided culture materials at reasonable cost, and I felt confident that I had the essentials of an adequate pediatric office.

A few weeks in the office, plus contacts with the visiting nurses, alerted me to significant numbers of patients who were in poverty. In order to save them money I would often tell a patient when I needed to follow up on an ear infection, for example, that I would be making house calls in his neighborhood. "Why don't I stop at your home to check that ear without any extra cost to you?" I'd say. In addition, I often asked for advice from the three other pediatricians in Bangor, and the four of us shared night and weekend calls.

At Eastern Maine General Hospital I was appointed to the medical records committee and the library committee. Dr. Lawrence Weed, a fine internist, was the only other member of the library committee; the two of us functioned well as a team to create an excellent reference library for the hospital. In this way I became acquainted with many of the staff, and thus stimulated a number of referrals. I was also involved with a health clinic for Penobscot Indians on Indian Island only a few miles away. A clinic for handicapped children offered another source of income, as did part-time employment as a school physician at the University of Maine, Orono.

One of my early house calls involved a family who gave me an address that appeared to be in the middle of a field. Disoriented, I asked for help from a neighbor at one end of the field. "Yes, there is a family living in that field; in that little hill is a potato house with a little door at the end." It was the home of the patient, partly below the ground, and with no windows. Needless to say, I did not charge, and was modest with future office charges.

Soon I was becoming quite busy and seeing complicated patients who taxed all of my abilities. One example is a child with aspirin poisoning. I admitted him to the hospital, where he had a very high salicylate (aspirin) level in his bloodstream. He needed a kidney dialysis to remove most of the circulating salicylate, but this equipment was not available at our hospital. I called Dr. Fred Emery, a fellow pediatrician, who recalled a recent article in the *Journal of Pediatrics* describing the use of an exchange transfusion to reduce the toxic salicylate level in the blood. I had performed such transfusions a number of times to reduce the bilirubin levels in newborns with Rh incompatibilities. Knowing that there was insufficient time to fly this semi-comatose child to Boston, I obtained permission from the family to perform this procedure, a lifesaving measure.

Dr. Emery read the instructions to me over the phone, and I proceeded without incident. Within two hours, the salicylate level was reduced by half and the child was wide awake and alert. Adequate hydration intravenously was effective in removing the rest of the salicylate as residual in his urine.

I encountered other serious illness, as in this house call on a child with a draining ear, while I was covering for one of the other pediatricians. The lad was already on an antibiotic. He exhibited fever and a stiff neck. Suspecting

meningitis, I immediately admitted him to the hospital. A spinal tap was compatible for meningitis, but no organisms were seen in the spinal fluid or in the
ear drainage. I had to guess, temporarily, that the cause was due to the most
common cause of meningitis in this age group, and treated him with the
appropriate antibiotics. Cultures the next morning showed no organisms, and
because the child was worse, I arranged to fly him to Boston for further
treatment. Two days later he died of tuberculous meningitis, which can only be
diagnosed with special bacterial stains for tuberculosis, which I did not suspect.

This experience was devastating to me, and realizing that I needed more
training regarding childhood tuberculosis, I left my practice for two weeks to
train with Dr. Edith Lincoln, the U.S. expert in childhood tuberculosis, at
Bellevue Hospital, New York City. I returned a better-trained pediatrician, for
I encountered a number of patients with childhood tuberculosis in northeastern Maine.

A serious problem for families living in older homes is lead poisoning.
Often, these homes are painted with paint containing lead, which causes
serious neurologic problems in those exposed to this toxin. I admitted a semi-
comatose child with possible brain damage from ingesting plaster in the walls
of his home. There was a high concentration of lead in his blood, and he
exhibited "lead lines" at the growing edges of his long bones on X-ray, where
they seem to light up in these areas. What, exactly, was the source of the lead?
There were some clues in the history. Apparently this child often chewed
material scraped from the walls near the kitchen table. I photographed the
area and took material for sampling, which showed high concentrations of
lead. Fortunately, with a process called de-leading of his blood, he recovered
with minimal neurologic damage. Paint had to be removed from the interior
walls of his home before he was allowed to return home.

I often had night house calls, which were especially tiring, for they
affected my performance on the following day. I never refused such calls,
although occasionally they were expensive for me, as in the following
example. It was two in the morning and as I was returning from a house call,
I saw no traffic and drove through two red lights and into my driveway to
find a police car parking immediately behind me. "May I see your license?
Oh, Doc, I didn't know that it was you. My wife takes her children to you.
Let this be a warning." My startled reply was, "You can't treat me any dif-
ferently from other drivers. I should have a ticket." He obligingly wrote me a
ticket!

One night I forgot to write down the name of the patient, and was rudely awakened an hour later, "Where are you, Doctor? I called you and you haven't arrived." Apologies were in order as I headed for the proper destination. Another "Yes, Mrs. ___, I will be right over," only to realize that I had forgotten to write the address. Rarely, after answering in the affirmative, I would fall right back asleep, only to encounter an angry patient recall. I learned quickly that the mind does not function well immediately after such a call, and it is best to write down names and addresses quickly, before preparing to leave for the visit. Sometimes in the middle of the next day, while taking a history in the office, a surprised parent would remind me, "Why Doctor, I believe you have fallen asleep."

The visiting nurses knew the neighborhoods well, knew the problems of many of the families. The nurses and I worked well together, for they found that established physicians were not anxious to add poor or partial families to their rolls. I was often asked to visit families with undernourished children, frequently a single mother trying to support one or more children on an inadequate income. Often they had no car, and because of this had no way of reaching a doctor. House calls provided a ready answer.

The patients were not the only ones having financial difficulty. We shared that problem. I did not send bills for the first six months in the belief that charges posted in the office would be adequate notice. This was not profitable. When I began to send bills, I improved my status, though not appreciably. At the end of my first year of practice, my annual income was minus fifty dollars, not an auspicious beginning for a young pediatrician. As a result, I stopped my credit card transactions, including fuel for my Volkswagen Beetle, and started a vegetable garden. I visited the offices of the local obstetricians to become better acquainted and worked closely with the nurse in charge of the newborn nurseries.

One child whom I had treated for a streptococcal sore throat developed a swollen ankle two weeks after treatment. Concerned, I made a house call and found a child who could not walk because of a swollen, very warm ankle, but no heart murmurs to indicate rheumatic heart disease. I took a repeat throat culture, and treated with a ten-day course of penicillin, which is the usual practice to prevent rheumatic fever. I visited several times to note that the swelling had subsided and the child showed no other findings suggesting rheumatic fever.

I carried a harmonica wherever I visited and discovered that it was ideal for frightened children. I never wore a white coat in the office. I always remembered birthdays, and, if in the office or in the home, played "Happy Birthday" for the unsuspecting child. Contacts with the local osteopaths were cordial, for in Bangor they handled much of the family practice responsibilities. One practitioner in particular was such a careful diagnostician that I rarely disagreed with his diagnoses, offering only confirmation or encouragement.

A doctor sent me a patient from Eastport, Maine, about one hundred miles away. A six-month-old child had a rash that did not respond to his treatment. I felt that the child had severe eczema, which would respond to my recommended treatment. Two months later, he called to tell me that my treatment was not working and sent the child to Children's Medical Center, Boston. They made a diagnosis of Letterer Siwe's disease, a rare illness with an eczematous rash but other features that I had overlooked. I was humbled by my incompetence, even though the doctor continued to send me other patients.

The child of a nurse showed normal development until age eight months. I noted that the head was growing too fast, but couldn't find the cause by an ordinary head X-ray. I placed a ventricular needle, which identified a firm mass. I arranged a trip to Children's Hospital, Boston, where a benign tumor was removed. The child recovered normally.

One infection that all pediatricians dread is meningococcus meningitis, or a meningococcus blood infection, called meningococcemia. While covering the emergency room at Eastern Maine General Hospital, I received a call from Ellsworth Hospital, thirty miles away, with a seriously ill teenager. Almost in a coma on arrival, he had a rash characteristic of meningococcemia, with so many of the bacteria in his bloodstream that the bacteriologist could see them on an ordinary blood smear. We administered emergency antibiotics appropriate for the infection, yet he died two hours after arrival. This is an infection that can affect any-age patient, though it occures more often in young individuals. The bacteria reproduce so rapidly that they may overwhelm the patient within the first twenty-four hours of the infection.

One evening a doctor from Millinocket, about seventy-five miles away, said he was bringing in a child with severe croup that had not responded to treatment. I met him in our emergency room in an hour when, much to his surprise, his patient was much improved. The child was so excited about the racetrack driver who sat next to him that he relaxed his breathing involuntarily. I reassured the physician that I had similar experiences with croup patients, and sent him home with some medication available from the emergency room, along with praise for his concern for the patient.

I had encountered a few childhood diabetics, always children difficult to treat adequately. Other physicians had similar experiences and prompted me to ask about a speaker on the subject for our local medical society. I knew just the person, Dr. Allan Butler, who taught me much about the subject at Massachusetts General Hospital. As our houseguest, he presented a concise overview of the topic that evening. During the question period he was engaged in a lively debate with Dr. Lawrence Weed, our director of medical education for the hospital. The men had differing views about the management of diabetic acidosis, which added to the drama of the evening.

Dr. Butler wanted to remain another day to see Eastern Maine General Hospital and my relationship to it. I showed him the pediatric floor, on the third level of the hospital. It was a large room, partitioned off by curtains about the beds as the only protection from the cries of other children. I told him that pediatrics was not a moneymaker for the hospital and thus was not on a high priority list for improvements. He commented favorably on Dr. Weed's and my efforts on behalf of the medical library.

When leaving for Boston, he left me with the admonition, "John, you shouldn't be here." Dr. Butler's words did not register with me at the time and were no more than a passing memory as I became involved with a busy practice.

Two or three weeks later, I began receiving phone calls from other parts of New England and even as far away as Rochester, New York. The callers were pediatricians who wanted another associate. I realized that Dr. Butler must have had something to do with this. One call in particular was impressive: "You don't know me, but I'm Dr. Paul Beaven from Rochester, New York. I'm planning to retire later this year and have two associates, all of us on the teaching staffs of the University Medical Center and several other Rochester Hospitals. It's a wonderful opportunity for a well-trained pediatrician."

Following a number of questions that he answered satisfactorily, I finally responded, "I don't believe I should move after only three years in Bangor. I still have much to do here." His reply: "I feel so sorry for you, John." As I pondered this, I wrestled with the decision for about fifteen minutes, then called him back: "Dr. Beaven, we would like to visit if we can both see you together," speaking for Dotty, also.

We flew to Rochester, visited for three days, and liked Dr. Beaven immensely (he was considered the dean of pediatricians in Rochester). We also liked his two partners, Dr. Fox, personable and friendly, and Dr.

Townsend, intense and respectable. "We have placed the responsibility for our sicker patients on ourselves," said Dr. Townsend, explaining that "we will make a house call the following morning unless the family calls and cancels. In this way we make certain that progress is satisfactory and that we have not overlooked a new finding that would jeopardize the patient."

Dotty and I were pleased with the possibilities in Rochester. Sharing a practice with two other physicians, I would not be on call every night, would have more opportunities to be with our family, and would not be responsible for office management, which was in the hands of an efficient administrator, who had been with the practice for over twenty years. Leaving Bangor would be somewhat traumatic for me, as I was not pleased with abandoning families who were dependent on me for their pediatric needs. In contrast, Dotty had found it a struggle to maintain a tiny budget, and to protect the family part of our home from inquisitive patients. Furthermore, she saw little of me even though we lived in the same house.

One of our favorite diversions, during our three years in Bangor, involved visiting the Hitchcock family, whom I had known since the age of ten. Now living fifty miles away in Southwest Harbor, bordering Acadia National Park on Mt. Desert Island, the Hitchcocks were living in one of the most picturesque and lovely areas on the East Coast. We visited on three weekends to say our good-byes. We knew that our move to New York State would allow only occasional visits.

My responsibility to my patients involved appropriate referrals to the three other pediatricians and making certain that their records were properly transferred and that good-byes to patients were not too unhappy. Our move occurred in the summer of 1958, which did not interrupt the school year for our children. We placed our modest home on the real estate market, though we realized that there would be difficulties with a somewhat static economy in Bangor at that time.

Rochester Programs

*T*he new practice was well organized and efficient, and revolved around our receptionist–office manager, Justine, who had been with Dr. Paul Beaven for many years. She knew most of the patients well, and scheduled our house calls with logical routes since she was familiar with most of the city streets. She was especially helpful to me in my adjustment to the office and call routine. Dr. Townsend and Dr. Fox were most accommodating to me as the youngest of our partnership. To them, house calls were an important part of the practice. Several examples will illustrate.

Dr. Townsend wanted me to accompany him on a trip to give a speech, but received a call from a mother whose crying child had phimosis, a tightening of the foreskin over a swollen penis. "Mrs. ___, I will be right over," he told her. We arrived in ten minutes. He reduced the phimosis and gave instructions to the mother to prevent a recurrence, leaving a happy mother and a contented baby. Both of us were on our way for the scheduled talk. Another mother recalled for me, "I called at three in the morning and told him that I just wanted reassurance. He was here in ten minutes and all three of us were in the hospital in half an hour. How did I know that my baby had meningitis?"

Dr. Townsend was a scholar and a brilliant pediatrician, yet found time to make the patient come first. Everything would be dropped if an emergency call came in. "If in doubt, see the patient," he taught. "Follow up, follow up, follow up," he advised, "for only in this way will you prevent an error in judgment. Remove a child's clothing at each visit, for it allows a complete examination regardless of the complaint." This advice helped me on a few occasions, when I discovered a skin rash that would not have been evident without my removing the child's clothing at the time of the visit.

One unanswered problem remained as a result of our move. There was little progress with the sale of our home in Bangor. After six months of no activity, I called the realtor and offered him a case of Johnny Walker's Black Label whiskey. "Each week the house is unsold, I will remove a bottle for myself, but the sooner the house is sold, the more bottles for you." The house was sold in two weeks, on Christmas Eve to a Mr. Christmas. The realtor called me that evening while I was on house calls. "Congratulations," I remarked, "I'll send you the remainder of the case this week." That same night, I was so excited that I left my stethoscope on a house call. At the next house the child appeared to have an upper respiratory infection, and I planned to do most of the examination without my stethoscope. When I explained that I could listen to the chest with my ear since the stethoscope is only the extension of the ear, the mother was shocked, "How can you really examine my child without your stethoscope?" I returned to the previous house, retrieved the forgotten stethoscope, and completed the examination, much to the satisfaction of this parent. The news reverberated to my colleagues, much to my embarrassment. This incident did not dampen my appreciation of a wonderful Christmas present, the sale of our home in Bangor.

I want to explain more about the importance of house calls to our practice. We told parents that they could expect a house call the morning after a child with high fever was seen in the office. Parents were free to call and cancel the call if the child was progressing as expected. "Please call us by seven AM to cancel since that is the time we start making calls," we instructed parents. Justine would, as our coordinator of our calls, notify each of us of any cancellations, or add new calls that came in during the morning. Often we made eight to ten house calls a morning, in addition to our hospital visits. I felt like a puppet, managed efficiently by Justine, whose judgment and efficiency were fine-tuned after years of experience.

One Christmas morning, I received a call at six AM. I was given a name but failed to ask the address, under the assumption that I knew the family well. I rang the doorbell and awakened a startled mother. "This is Christmas morning and none of my children are sick."

"Someone with your name called about thirty minutes ago," I commented.

"Oh, that's probably one of our relatives two streets over." I sheepishly called at the proper home in a few minutes.

Other mistaken identities occurred, as in this call. "Doctor, please come. Our apartment is upstairs; go through the back door and don't bother to knock." I walked up the stairs and followed instructions not to knock and was met by a startled woman whom I had never seen before.

"Who are you?" she asked.

"I'm Dr. Radebaugh, and I came to see your sick child."

"What number were you planning to visit?"

"One-eighty-three."

"Oh, that's two houses down the street."

Profuse apologies were in order.

Snowstorms provided additional drama on house calls. Rochester is in the snowbelt from Lake Erie and Lake Ontario storms, which can drop a foot of snow within a few hours. With a Volkswagen Beetle, usually a good snow car, I felt confident. It was another Christmas Eve, and I was asked to see a child who lived close to Lake Ontario, some distance from our home. A blizzard was in process. Visibility was so bad that I could not see the road, but luckily, I was able to follow closely behind a snowplow until we approached the address that I wanted; I was quickly able to find the home. After examining the child and initiating treatment, the family told me, "Doctor, you can't leave in this blizzard. Stay and watch Victor Borge with us on TV." I watched the whole show, chuckling all the way, at the end of which the blizzard had subsided enough for me to leave.

Another blizzard brought me to another home close to the shores of Lake Ontario. A child was huddled in a blanket on the sofa, not far from a window that had been broken by gale-force winds. I initiated treatment, with plans to follow up during the next morning, but the child improved in spite of the less than ideal home conditions.

During a January blizzard, this one lasting two days, I was asked at seven PM to see a child with an asthma attack. I thought that I could weather the storm with the fairly well-plowed roads in Rochester, but this was not the case in Henrietta, where this child lived. Soon I was mired in one of the extensive drifts and had to abandon my car. A passing Jeep driver offered me a ride, but his vehicle foundered in a large snowdrift. "My house is only a short walk from here. You are welcome to stay there as long as you need," he said.

After a short time, well warmed again, I called the home I was to visit. "My car is mired in a snowdrift, but I'll find a way to your home. Don't worry."

After thanking my host, I faced the fiercely blowing wind and snow, wearing a heavy overcoat and hat, inherited from my father. I walked along the road for a quarter of a mile and saw the lights of a house immediately ahead. I knocked on the door, with the hope of warming myself before continuing. The door opened, and an elderly couple, spotting this snow-covered apparition on the doorstep, immediately closed and locked the door. Undaunted, I trudged ahead until I encountered a snowplow, asked for a ride to the next road, the site of the address of the asthmatic child, and paid five dollars to the accommodating driver. The mother met the snow-covered ghostlike snowman. Removing my snowy coat, I apologized for my tardiness. "Doctor, Joey was so excited about your coming through the blizzard that he has been looking out the window constantly for your arrival. I don't understand why he has stopped wheezing." Indeed, he was much better than the description I had received over the telephone a few hours before.

I replied: "Sometimes distracting an asthmatic can relieve some of the anxiety. I can understand why he is better. Have him take this medicine to prevent further problems."

I telephoned the N.Y. state police barracks, which were nearby, and asked for assistance to reach my home. An hour later, about one in the morning, I was deposited at my home, exhausted from what was to have been a simple house call. I slept till late in the morning, then shoveled a safe exit out of the driveway. Dressed warmly, I took a snow shovel, and a neighbor drove me to the supposed location of my car in Henrietta. I could not find it until, suddenly, I spotted the tip of a radio aerial in a snowdrift. After an hour of shoveling, I exposed the Volkswagen, its front door dented where a snowplow had pushed it aside. A kick on the inside of the door removed the dent and I was on my way home, having survived a harrowing evening and a struggling day to retrieve my car. My bravado through a number of such storms gave me great respect for the power of wind and snow to frustrate even the best of intentions.

Occasionally I became too tired to function efficiently. "Doctor, you look exhausted this late at night. We can offer you the living room sofa for a catnap before you drive home." Sometimes I took such an offer only to find myself waking three or four hours later. Sometimes I was too tired to drive safely, and on one night with three house calls to complete before midnight, I drove off the street onto a sidewalk before waking. Frightened, I found a pay phone and called a taxi to complete the remaining three calls, even though the cab fare far exceeded the usual house call fees. I did not want to experience the same dangerous situation again, and fortunately, I was able to hire a neighborhood high school student to become my chauffeur for some of those late-night calls.

Occasional house calls can be lifesaving. Our morning house call lists are responses to phone message needs as described by parents. One morning, my list included a child with croup, whom I scheduled as the first on my list, not suspecting a serious problem. Upon arrival at the home, I realized that this child was in extreme distress, struggling to breathe, and was in much more difficulty than the usual child with croup. I had suspected epiglottitis, an infection that blocks the airway because of a swollen epiglottis, a serious emergency. The epiglottis is a small flap of tissue separating the esophagus from the windpipe, or trachea. There wasn't time to wait for an ambulance, so I telephoned the emergency room, and I bundled the mother and child into my car and drove, horn blowing, to the University Hospital emergency room, a short distance from the home. An ear, nose, and throat specialist and an anesthesiologist met me at the door and, recognizing the problem, took the child immediately to the operating room. The anesthesiologist inserted an endotracheal tube to provide a temporary airway, at which time the child went into a deep sleep, relieved from his severe efforts at breathing. The ear, nose, and throat doctor performed a tracheotomy, a small opening into the front of the neck that allows the insertion of a special airway tube.

The tube was removed in four days, after the swelling of the epiglottis subsided. Epiglottitis may be caused by a virus, as occurs rarely with mumps, or a bacterium, hemophilus influenza or diphtheria, the latter associated with many deaths in the past. Early childhood immunizations now prevent diphtheria.

During a flu epidemic, we made many house calls on patients with high fevers. One such patient prompted me to return the following morning. A new finding, a stiff neck in this feverish child, caused me to take mother and child immediately to the emergency room where a spinal tap revealed findings of early meningitis, which resolved with immediate treatment. Dr. Townsend's advice about "follow up, follow up, follow up" was fortunate in relation to this child.

Some emergencies are so sudden that a house call may be too late, as in this call: "Doctor, my baby has stopped breathing, and my husband has the car." "I will be there as fast as I can." I telephoned for a police escort, but my effort to keep pace with the more powerful police cruiser was impossible for my small Volkswagen, though we did reach the house in record time. The four-month-old baby was dead, a victim of "sudden infant death syndrome," which may occur in previously healthy, vigorous babies. I could do nothing but try to comfort the grieving mother. At autopsy, no definitive cause was evident, as is characteristic of this syndrome.

I had a similar experience when receiving a call from a drugstore near our office at 26 South Goodman St. I was there in a few minutes, only to find a distraught mother holding her dead baby while standing next to her car. She said that she left her baby in the car while she made a quick errand to the drugstore. She returned to find her baby not breathing and was certain that the baby had smothered under her blanket. I reassured her that it was not her fault, but due to sudden infant death syndrome. Again, autopsy findings were inconclusive. Many years later, the incidence of sudden infant death syndrome has decreased by having infants sleep on their back rather than on their stomach.

Unsuspected events frequently present themselves on house calls. For example, I was visiting a sick child when I noted a pistol in a holster nailed to the wall over the kitchen table. No adult was home at the time, but later I visited to admonish the father about the danger of handguns in the home; he did remove it and, I hope, got rid of it. I have had a fear of hand weapons ever since my experiences in World War II, coupled with reports of accidental deaths from hand guns in the home.

Some of our patients had cystic fibrosis, a hereditary disease associated with thickened secretions that obstruct airways in the lungs, causing bacteria to multiply. They were living in mist tents at home to allow increased humidity needed to help liquefy their secretions. We were called frequently to check on their lungs and the adequacy of antibiotic treatments, if indicated. This helped our patients avoid unnecessary office or hospital visits, although Dr. Townsend and I, especially, were involved along with the visiting nurses in the home care of these patients.

In a well-organized office, Dr. Townsend noted that some home visits were best performed by nurses than by physicians, especially in relation to newborn babies recently discharged from the hospital. He assigned one of our most skilled nurses to visit the same day or on subsequent days until the mother was relaxed with her new baby. This saved a number of phone calls by anxious parents.

Among the many surprises encountered during house calls was this: I visited a child whose parents were both working. I found the child watching two TV programs at the same time on parallel sets—a simultaneous double feature. His mother left a telephone number to call with my instructions for treatment.

Though a general pediatric office deals with many common pediatric illnesses, it is occasionally involved with unusual, even rare diseases, as for example:

Following a normal delivery, a baby developed a series of convulsions with collapse, irregular breathing, and cyanosis (blueness). A spinal fluid analysis was normal except for very low sugar levels. Blood sugars were unusually low for an infant, and subsequent blood sugar analyses were also very low. We had to give the baby constant intravenous infusions in order to maintain a normal blood sugar. When these were interrupted, the infant promptly had a convulsion. Apparently, this infant was producing too much insulin from his pancreas, and a few weeks after birth, a surgeon performed a partial pancreatectomy, which corrected the problem but for just two weeks.

Finally, we instituted feedings every three hours around the clock to prevent low blood sugars, but this was especially difficult for his mother, who was responsible for the care of three other children. A month later we noted that the infant was not growing normally, indicating a possible lack of growth hormone from the pituitary gland (at the base of the brain). At that time, growth hormone was available only from human pituitary glands, usually obtained from hospital autopsies. For the next year, I collected pituitary glands from autopsies performed throughout the Rochester area, and sent them, frozen, to a research scientist in Boston. He extracted the growth hormone and sent half to me and kept the other half.

Upon receipt of the hormone, I began house calls for this child to administer a small shot of human growth hormone three times weekly. Soon, I transferred this responsibility to the visiting nurses, but saw him in our office every two weeks to observe his progress. Within a month he began to show significant growth. The parents and I were overjoyed, especially since he began to show consistently normal blood sugars, related to the regular injections of growth hormone. During the next year, he showed progressive growth with normal blood sugars. Though low blood sugars can be associated with brain damage, there was no evidence with extensive psychometric testing that damage had occurred.

The family moved to Buffalo, New York, where I referred them to a fine endocrinologist who monitored his course for a number of years. The patient moved to Pennsylvania, where I learned that he had grown to five feet seven inches, slightly below that of his male siblings, but certainly an acceptable height.

In the early 1960s, other events occurred in the Rochester area, related to the larger civil rights movement under the leadership of Martin Luther King Jr. There was considerable discrimination against African-American employees at Eastman Kodak Company, the largest employer in the city of Rochester. African-Americans were relegated to mediocre positions at Kodak. Fight, a civil rights organization headed by an African-American minister,

Rev. Franklin Florence, was attempting to correct conditions there. Saul Alinsky, who had stimulated effective changes in Chicago as an advocate for human rights, was a consultant to Fight. Meanwhile, Rev. Franklin Florence and his family had received threats against their lives, causing his wife to be worried about the safety of their children.

I treated their children for a few illnesses, and during the ensuing year we developed a trusting relationship. As an active member of the Asbury Methodist Church in Rochester, I was asked to help plan for brotherhood Sunday. I thought that Minister Florence and his congregation would be appropriate participants, and he agreed to do so. When I presented tentative plans to our minister, I met with complete opposition.

"This will split our congregation completely in half, since many of our members are Kodak employees. You cannot do this to us, John. You will have to cancel."

"Sir, I cannot go back on my word. Whites are known to speak with forked tongues when it comes to agreements with African-Americans."

For half an hour we debated the question. I insisted that refusal would be degrading for Reverend Florence and for his congregation.

"Isn't this supposed to be Brotherhood Sunday?"

"We must have an emergency meeting of the board to decide this issue," my minister replied.

I approached the board meeting with fear, but I tried to present the rationale for us to be gracious hosts. The vote was close, and by one vote we were allowed to proceed with plans. Our minister insisted that Franklin Florence preach in the early service, usually attended by a few Sunday school teachers and church members. We were surprised by events at the time of Brotherhood Sunday.

The sanctuary was filled completely with attendees and members of Minister Florence's congregation. He delivered his sermon in an effective and moving fashion, and impressed our church members profoundly. One month later, the church started a day care program for inner-city families, many of whom were African-American.

Shortly after Brotherhood Sunday, and with the advice of Mr. Alinsky, Minister Florence and Fight confronted Eastman Kodak with demonstrations, and well-publicized meetings that gained the support of the local newspaper and many community leaders. As a result, medium-level job opportunities were offered African-Americans and even included several vice presidential appointments. The Fight director was soon accepted by the

Rochester community, and threats against his family evaporated. The University of Rochester Medical School appointed an African-American physician from the faculty to become the director of a new community medicine program in the inner city. Though this initial progress was clearly evident, it was recognized as only an early step to improve racial relations in Rochester.

At the same time, I was experiencing some changes at the medical school. I presented a report about the child I had been treating with hypoglycemia and growth arrest due to a growth hormone defect. A Johns Hopkins Medical School faculty member was present. Shortly after the presentation, I was offered an interview at that medical school for a position on the faculty. My wife and I visited twice and decided not to accept the offer. Later, I received a similar offer to join the Rochester pediatric faculty under the chairmanship of Dr. Robert Haggerty, whom I admired for his innovative leadership. I enjoyed the exciting possibility to become an academic faculty member, and with many regrets to our staff, announced my decision. I was especially indebted to Dr. Townsend, who as the senior member of our trio had taught me many of the finer points of pediatrics.

As a junior faculty member, I was involved with chronic diseases, including pediatric arthritis, cystic fibrosis, hemophilia, and pediatric rehabilitation, the latter in a newly established rehabilitation unit at the hospital. I was starting on the lowest rung of the academic ladder, and several experiences are worthy of comment:

An excellent pediatrician in a nearby community sent us a child with a swollen tender knee, which was very warm and painful, but he seemed to be healthy otherwise. The admitting diagnosis was mono-articular rheumatoid arthritis (one joint involved). After several days of examinations and study, I felt that the child did, indeed, have rheumatoid arthritis. I returned the patient to his doctor with suggestions for treatment, which was unsuccessful. The physician performed a biopsy of the swollen joint and established a diagnosis of an unsuspected complication of a silent tumor, metastatic neuroblastoma. This tumor of the very young may arise in many areas of the neural tissue in the body, most commonly near the adrenal gland. The first symptoms may occur in the metastastic lesion, as in this unfortunate child. The final diagnosis was a complete surprise to me, but a tribute to the referring physician, who later chaired the Department of Pediatrics when Dr. Haggerty left for another position.

In the pediatric rehabilitation unit, we admitted a ten-year-old African-American girl who had been burned in the face and chest from a flash fire while she was cooking breakfast for two younger siblings. Her mother had gone to work and left her ten-year-old daughter in charge of the younger siblings. In preparing to discuss her treatment plans, I had diagrammed her burns in percentages on the blackboard. She walked up to the blackboard, erased the diagram, and wrote her name. Our neglect of her psychological needs was evident by her dramatic response. She was an actual person and not a series of percentages on the blackboard.

I was fully involved with hospital responsibilities, yet within a few miles from Rochester another population was neglected by the medical school and the hospital. Naomi Chamberlain, an African-American faculty member in the Department of Community Medicine, introduced that population to a few of us, whom she invited to visit some of the migrant worker camps in surrounding communities. I knew nothing about migrant farm workers, but immediately endured eye-opening experiences in the camps. In addition to primitive living conditions, unsafe water supplies, inadequate toilet facilities, no screening, and very little privacy, they had no medical care. We were shocked that such primitive conditions existed on farms in the Rochester environs.

Naomi Chamberlain offered to help us organize an evening clinic on one of the farms and within a few weeks we had enough supplies and volunteers to conduct a small clinic at Martin Farm in Brockport, about twenty-five miles west of Rochester. We opened this clinic in August 1965. The program quickly expanded to two night clinics per week, staffed by nurses, medical students, and several medical faculty under the leadership of Naomi Chamberlain. At the end of each clinic, we reviewed with the staff and students the problems we encountered, a unique teaching program on the premises. By the end of the summer, we had an understanding of the workers' multiple problems, the role of crew bosses, and the attitudes of the local doctors and workers.

As the harvest season came to a close, we encountered referral problems to some of the home areas, in Florida, of returning migrants. This is one glaring example: I sent a letter to the Florida Health Department about a child who required a hernia repair but was leaving for Florida the next day. I received in return a brief note scribbled on my letter, "Sorry, we have no facilities to take care of this child." We never learned the fate of that child.

The following year, the owner of a nearby farm with a large worker population offered a building that we could use as a medical clinic. He volunteered to alter the interior of the building to be better utilized for medical purposes. Clinics were held evenings twice weekly there, with increasing numbers of farm workers compared to a year ago. One of the staff made occasional house calls to some of the cement-block homes of nearby workers. On a September evening we received a call to visit a woman in labor. Accompanied by an internist and two nursing students, I found a woman in obvious labor. We did not examine her but instead bundled her into my car and drove hurriedly to the hospital emergency room. While assisting her into a wheelchair, I was soaked when her membranes ruptured. We left her with the obstetric personnel and headed home.

The next morning I called to check on her progress. "Oh, she isn't here; she was discharged last night."

"How could you do that?" I questioned.

"She wasn't in labor. She just had a full bladder and has pseudocyesis."

Not appearing to be completely ignorant, I discontinued the conversation and looked up the diagnosis: "a false pregnancy," usually occurring in women in emotional stress or with a strong desire to become pregnant. The ruptured membranes were the result of inadvertent emptying of her bladder on a cold evening (too cold to use the outhouse). For about a week, the other doctor and I were the laughingstock of the hospital.

Conditions in many of the camps were intolerable, with no screening, overutilized toilets to overflowing, contaminated water supplies so that workers had to walk long distances for adequate water, and no toilet facilities in the fields. Crew bosses sold liquor for high prices in the camps and deducted pay for trivial items. As a result, many workers were discouraged, and wanted to return to Florida before the end of the season. Realizing that conditions would not improve without definitive action, we developed a plan. With the assistance of several of our staff, we called for a city bus visit to the camp where our clinic was located. This bus took workers to Rochester, where they were met by two social workers to direct them to rooms at the top floor of one of the hotels. On the following morning a larger bus, with an accompanying social worker, waited to take them back to Florida. This was reported in dramatic fashion by the Rochester newspapers, to the ire of the growers in the area, and especially the camp owner, who immediately closed our clinic. Other actions followed quickly.

Arthur Hardwick Jr., a New York senator from Buffalo, was the chairman of the New York State Senate Committee on Migrant Farm Workers. He took me on a house call to one of the Orleans County farms. Workers were housed in an abandoned three-story chicken coop, which featured whitewashed walls covered with chicken excreta. Other nearby camps showed ill-functioning stoves, holes in walls between rooms, and overflowing toilet facilities, all conditions that should cause local health departments to condemn and close such facilities. But this never happened, according to Senator Hardwick, who complained bitterly to the local newspapers and openly criticized the local health commissioners. The efforts of Arthur Hardwick Jr., an African-American, were remarkable.

His previous experiences as a migrant worker gave him insights and methods not available to most legislators. Dressed as a migrant worker, he asked for employment on an Orleans County farm. The grower hired him, but offered pay much less than the New York State minimum wage. He worked for a half day and quit his job, only to return two weeks later with his full committee to inspect the camp. When he confronted the grower, he was dressed in business clothing, and queried:

"Do you recognize me?" The grower denied any recognition.

"I am the same worker whom you hired two weeks ago at less than the minimum wage. I quit work that same day." A curtain suddenly lifted from the face of the grower.

"I am chairman of the New York State Senate Committee on Migrant Farm Workers, and these men are members of my committee. We are going to have you indicted for failure to obey New York State laws regarding fair wages for migrant workers." More was accomplished under Mr. Hardwick's chairmanship than by any previous Senate committee overseeing migrant workers.

Meanwhile, I made a house call on a farm in nearby Wayne County and interviewed a number of farm workers, one of whom showed me a ten-cent check for two weeks of work. Deductions were so unfair that the worker had no money available for food or other personal needs. I photographed the check, made a 35-mm slide, and showed this, along with the slides of some of the unbelievable conditions on some of the nearby farms, to Senator Harrison Williams's U.S. Senate Committee on migrant farm worker problems. In the fall of 1968, Senator Robert Kennedy, as a result of that testimony, asked me to pick two camps for him to inspect a few weeks later. He was accompanied by newspaper reporters and Senator Jacob Javits of New York. The grower met the entourage with a shotgun and Senator Kennedy asked a nearby worker to invite him to visit his home. The surprised grower could only stand in amazement as Senators Kennedy and Javits, along with a large entourage of reporters, walked to the abode, an unheated school bus without an engine.

"Why are you wearing only one shoe?" Mr. Kennedy asked the worker.

"Rats ate the other shoe last night," answered the worker.

As they inspected this, one of the many school bus homes, and the surrounding land, they found human excrement surrounding some of the unusable outhouses, absent doors on some of the school buses, some of the most deplorable conditions that Senators Kennedy and Javits had ever seen. That afternoon the senators held hearings in a Rochester courthouse and severely criticized the growers, with reporters eagerly reporting events. The growers knew that I was involved with this investigation, about which I was to hear more later.

Not all farm workers migrated, and a few settled in to old school buses without motors or wheels, or in simple house trailers, usually heated with kerosene stoves. These may be associated with fires, some fatal. On February 27, 1968, I received a phone call immediately after such an accident. The migrant farm worker who died was employed on one of the farms where we had developed a clinic. Similar accidents occurred at least once each winter.

One of the workers in one of the camps had a more encouraging experience. She wanted to remain in this area with her only child. In October, she was living in an unheated cement-block apartment. The cement floors were very cold, transmitting that through my shoes. It was obvious that she could not remain in the camp through the winter. With the help of a social worker, we were able to locate a small apartment near a community health center in Rochester. As an African-American, she had many helpful neighbors, and was overjoyed at a new life for herself and her daughter.

As a result of my testimony before the U.S. Senate migrant committee, a hearing that included the ten-cent check, and my involvement with the inspection by Senators Kennedy and Javits, the Wayne County growers, and doctors, demanded that I be dismissed from the medical school faculty. The dean suggested that I meet with them, discuss our differences, and try to develop a solution that was acceptable to all. I met with them on several occasions, one person among a roomful of angry doctors and growers who wanted me to apologize in public. In addition, they wanted me to know that one source of my data was a migrant worker who was unreliable. I agreed to draft a letter with the help of the dean and Dr. Haggerty, chairman of the Department of Pediatrics. I took the letter in person to the president of the Wayne County Medical Society. Though the letter was not completely

University of Rochester migrant clinic (1968)

satisfactory, it offered an opportunity for further dialogue. I was not dismissed from the medical school, but was cautioned to curb the community action by finding a constructive way to improve worker conditions.

Some of the most exploited workers were employed by the mink farms in Newark, New York, about thirty miles east of Rochester. Mink farm owners transported Indians from Canada in the fall of the year to skin mink for the fur coat trade. They were skilled experts, but spoke only their own dialects and were not considered citizens of Canada or of the United States. The farm owners paid them with tickets, which were turned in to the owners at the end of the short season. Isolated, they were unable to leave the premises, and had great difficulty receiving any health care. Learning of some of their problems, I visited their camp and examined a man who had broken his arm two weeks previously but had received no treatment. I arranged care for him at the University Hospital, and the farm owner transported him. I realized only too vividly the problems of these unfortunate workers.

During the next two years, the clinics increased in numbers, as did their patients. More volunteers participated, and we now had enough grant funds to hire several full-time employees. One of these was a superb African-American nurse who was placed in charge of one of the busiest clinics. She was well respected by the farm workers, and created a caring and efficient presence in the clinics. In fact she was often consulted first by many of the workers. Most of the staff emulated her attitude, and with her involvement, the nursing participation was considered the greatest asset of the clinics, much to my satisfaction.

Naomi Chamberlain developed a health education program for medical and nursing students to reach out to workers. She soon included some of the farm workers to become part-time staff members to increase the effectiveness of the program. Her organizing skills were invaluable to involve students and farm workers to play an active role in the health program.

The value of the health program is obvious with this one patient: A child with a high fever was seen in a nearby emergency room, with no available physician. The nurse on duty gave a shot of penicillin for an upper respiratory infection. Since the child was no better on the following day, the family sought help from the farm worker clinic, which they knew was open that evening. The child was diagnosed with meningitis and was immediately hospitalized at University Hospital and treated successfully. Had there been no clinic for two nights, it is possible that this child would have succumbed to the original illness. We felt that in the future, we should dovetail clinics, possibly on a nightly basis.

One unusual feature of the University of Rochester Migrant Health Program was the inclusion of a significant dental component. This was organized by Richard Beane, D.D.S., an African-American faculty member of the Eastman School of Dentistry. He enlisted the help of dental faculty, dental students, and even some private dentists to provide exemplary dental services. Here is a summary of his report:

"I recall working in a variety of locations, including schools, local private dental offices, and in some of the farm worker clinics. Most often we had to transport our equipment, instruments and supplies to the locations where the migrants were working. This included a large number of sterile instruments, such as forceps for extractions and instruments for operative procedures. Using mobile dental equipment and transporting these to sites was challenging. The dental units were packaged in a compact case and included hand pieces (drills) and a compressor unit to produce air pressure to operate the hand pieces. The same type of equipment was used by the military, as we worked in small rural communities with limited resources.

"There was a great need for services in the migrant population, which ordinarily had no access to dental care. There was much untreated dental disease, which meant that many teeth were not salvageable, especially in adults. Consequently, we extracted a lot of teeth, treated dental abscesses and treated many patients with acute and chronic dental pain. Yet, we filled a lot of teeth and were able to provide a large number of patients, especially the young ones, with reasonable dental health. I remember many evenings when patients filled the waiting rooms and were lined up along the walls waiting for service. We worked virtually nonstop until late in the evening before packing up and driving back to Rochester, exhausted.

"There was one memorable night with three young white women in the car. We were all dead tired, when we were stopped by a state police officer. He was curious about this black man driving a car full of white ladies. Our explanation satisfied him that we were on a credible mission, and he allowed us to continue our trip.

"I remember fondly the invaluable help of my young assistants who worked daily to organize the instruments, keep the records and provide secretarial functions. F.E. and D.B. were invaluable employees who worked overtime to ready supplies and equipment for the evening dental program."

Echoing his thoughts, I appreciated that Dr. Beane's staff was an important contribution to fill a serious need for migrant workers. In addition, the Rochester Migrant Health Program was successful in obtaining small grants to pay dentists for the use of their offices, to obtain necessary supplies, and to pay small travel expenses to and from clinics.

Soon, we received requests for consultations from other programs to help them receive funds. In addition to requests from the shade tobacco growers from Connecticut and a community medicine program in North Carolina, I received a request from California legal assistance lawyers to consult regarding a new program for workers in Imperial County in the desert close to the Mexican border. Brawley, a small town, was to be the site of the proposed clinic. We planned evening meetings in a room with a blackboard, and I supplied stethoscopes and an otoscope to familiarize workers with some of our medical equipment. Workers gave their version of what they wanted in a health program, which included a director, nurses, and three doctors, one of whom would be a bone specialist because of the frequency of limb and joint injuries. They wanted some farm workers to be part of the staff, and care to be available around the clock, weekends, and holidays. Above all, they requested a governing board consisting mostly of farm workers with one outside medical representative. After five days of data gathering, I returned to Rochester to incorporate these suggestions in a three-day marathon of grant writing. I sent this application to Casa de Amistad, one of the sponsoring organizations, requesting that they modify in any way they wished.

The odd hours of work with the migrant clinics, often with many nights away from home, began to have adverse effects on our family. I tried to make weekends available by being involved in skiing, exploring Rochester and nearby parks with Dotty and our children, and playing tennis with them, among other activities. Complicating our living was the threat of nuclear bombing from Russia, creating a near hysteria among many families, including ours. Our government suggested that people build home bomb shelters, and some of our neighbors did that. To reassure our children, I arranged for a truck-load of cement blocks to be delivered at our house, which the children carried into our cellar, supposedly to build a shelter. They were so entertained by building and rebuilding forts or other buildings that we never did accomplish a permanent structure. Nevertheless, this relieved some of the tension, especially with our older son, who lived alone on the third floor of our home.

In 1966, Biafrans in eastern Nigeria had declared independence from the rest of the nation. This was the result of massacres of Biafrans who were residing in northern Nigeria, with estimates as many as thirty thousand dead. Most of the surviving Biafrans returned to their home territory of southeastern Nigeria, which also contained the largest oil reserves in Africa. The Nigerian army expected a quick conquest of the secessionists, but this was not the case. In a long war, the Biafrans were surrounded by the better-armed Nigerian troops. In addition, the Nigerians were supplied with Russian MIG fighter planes, Egyptian pilots for the MIGs, and British weapons. The embattled Biafrans were short of food supplies after several years, and were dying of starvation in increasing numbers.

In January 1969, concerned about the largest genocide in the world since the Holocaust during World War II, I felt that by volunteering to offer services as a pediatrician in refugee camps for Biafran children, I could help save the lives of a few of these victims. I volunteered to join Operation Medicorps, funded partly by Rochester. Dr. Robert Haggerty, chairman of the Department of Pediatrics, understood my concern and allowed a brief leave of absence for this purpose, and coverage was available temporarily for my clinical responsibilities.

My flight from New York to Dakar, Senegal, with a connecting flight to Abidjan, Ivory Coast, was uneventful, and I was soon immersed in the French-speaking culture of a modern city. After checking with government

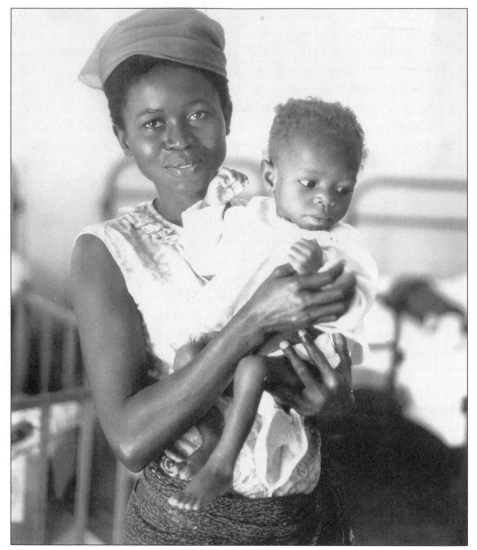

Biafran nurse with patient (1968)

officials, I was told that a plane from Biafra was due that day. It landed and during the next two hours the passengers were allowed to stretch while the plane was cleaned. Children in varying stages of disease showed for the most part pot-bellies, thin extremities, red hair, numerous skin sores, and swollen feet, characteristic of children with kwashiorkor, or protein deficiency disease. When the plane had been cleaned, much of the mess due to many children with diarrhea, the children were returned to the plane for the flight to

Bouake, a few hundred miles to the north, where I would see them again in a few days.

I met the director of Croix Rouge, the Ivorian Red Cross. He was my immediate supervisor and in charge of the construction of the three refugee camps for Biafran children. One was completed in Bouake, another was in process in Abidjan, and another was in the planning stages in Yamoousoukro. I was instructed to meet a doctor Rose from Philadelphia General Hospital. He was to return to the United States on my arrival. He was popular with the Biafrans and with the Ivorians, who did much of the cooking. He noticed that many of the undernourished children were not responding adequately to the meals, until he learned that meats, milk, and vitamins prescribed for the children were missing from their plates. The Ivorian staff did not share a concern for the children, who were getting better food and medical care than was available to the staff. Most lived in poverty and meat was a luxury for them, as was milk, and medical care was often not available. More careful supervision on our part remedied this problem and the children exhibited progress in their appearance and weight gain.

Malnutrition complicates infectious diseases, especially tuberculosis and measles, the latter a dreaded complication among the Biafran children. Five children developed measles and through the World Health Organization we were able to immunize the remaining children to stop the spread. A child with measles was placed in the isolation ward one day; one day later he developed pneumonia and, though treated vigorously with antibiotics, died on the third day. Autopsy (performed by me) showed pneumonia of all lobes of the lung. There were two other deaths before the epidemic subsided.

A number of children were treated for tuberculosis and many had chronic intestinal parasitic infections with resulting diarrhea. Stool exams revealed a variety of worms. Sanitation was a major problem and diarrhea stools were often on the floors. Flies were so prevalent that children could not keep them from their food, and the flies bothered them relentlessly when the youngsters tried to sleep.

Because of the number of sick children, some of whom had to be on intravenous treatments, a doctor was in the infirmary at all times, including all night. Some children had large livers from malaria; others had congestive heart failure, presumably from inadequate dietary protein; and most had scabies (a skin parasite), which they were constantly scratching. We had to send for emergency supplies of the medication for that condition.

The Biafran nurses who arrived with the children on the planes were well trained, as were the Irish, English, French, and Swiss nurses who had volunteered. Several were so skilled that they sewed lacerations and performed minor surgery. One nurse taught a doctor to repair rectal prolapse, a condition common in children with prolonged diarrhea.

As children improved, they responded to adult visitors by hugging their legs, or crawled onto laps as they sought affection. Once, when I sat to watch a movie with the children, I found myself cradling a half-dozen in my arms, with others on my lap and a few hugging my legs, eventually falling asleep and giving me a warm inner feeling that care was more important than medicines.

The camp at Cocody near Abidjan opened in February 1969, and within two weeks the staff of doctors and nurses became an effective team to care for these children. Barriers of language, nationality, and race were forgotten. In the case of the Biafran children, there was a strong will to survive, and there were those who wanted to assist to make that possible. It was really great to be a part of such a team.

Children, during the past few weeks, had been so desperately ill that we thought they would never live. One of them especially, a small child about two years old but appearing much younger, was only bones and loose skin from his chronic diarrhea. Intravenous treatments had to be continued for two weeks, with close attention from the Biafran nurses and the Ivorian monitresses (health aides). Eventually he was able to sit up in bed, gained weight, and looked more like a toddler. There were others, including some with measles for whom I had not much hope, who did survive.

To see older children carrying younger children to the dining hall or feeding them in their rooms, or to find a small wandering child and return him to his dormitory, gave me a sense of community and purpose to all that was happening. Who is able to fathom the depth of feeling in these children with the uncertainties of the future? Did they have families still waiting for them in Biafra? They lived in the present, but what would the future bring?

War is so devastating that the mere sound of planes flying overhead can cause an immediate cessation of playing or eating while children anxiously await their passing. Psychiatric problems occurred in some, and in a few cases, transfer to a nearby children's facility was necessary. How many would be delayed because of long-standing mental effects? The love that we as physicians and nurses and health aides offered was only a Band-Aid covering deeper traumas.

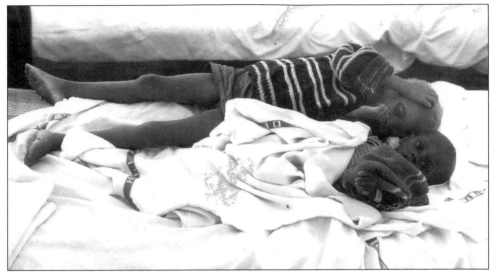

Family ties: two brothers together constantly

When I left, I realized that I was returning to a safe and loving home, while those children faced many uncertainties and losses. When one has been relating to such marvelous children, one wonders what has been accomplished by man's inhumanity to man. When will we ever learn?

A positive note: Many teachers accompanied the children, and any child over five years of age was enrolled in a schooling program. Along with classroom teaching, they learned traditional singing and dancing, manners, art, and games to maintain normality despite shortages of materials. The teachers, in addition to the nurses and doctors, were an important part of this cultural effort. The children returned gradually to spontaneous playfulness, so characteristic of happy children worldwide.

To return home after seven weeks in Africa was heartwarming, but I did not anticipate the profound effect on my family. None of my almost daily letters home had arrived, nor had any letters from home during the time I was in Côte d'Ivoire. The intense worries of my family, who saw frequent headlines about conditions in Biafra but nothing about conditions in the Ivory Coast, were profound. In addition, Dotty was involved as a passenger in an auto accident that left her bedridden for two weeks.

I gradually adjusted to the return, and spent more time with Dotty and our children, especially since the demands of night clinics decreased during the winter and spring. I concentrated on pediatric duties with the variety of programs under my supervision, and was able to be home most evenings. George, our older son, was enrolled as a freshman at Antioch College, Ohio, and Alan was accepted at Wooster College, also in Ohio. Susan was still in high school, in her junior year.

A few months later, the scene would suddenly shift, as I received the following telegram:

> Dr. John F. Radebaugh, Director of Migrant Health Project, University of Rochester School of Medicine:
>
> IT'S OFFICIAL. WE ARE FUNDED FOR JULY FIRST. A DAY TO CELEBRATE. WE ARE ALL WAITING FOR YOU, VIVA LA CAUSA. LA CLINICA, GILBERT LOPEZ

The telegram was associated with my consultation regarding a potential farm worker clinic in Brawley, California. The recipients of funding wanted me to join them if monies were awarded, and I had agreed that this was a possibility. For our family, it was a huge change from the cool Rochester climate to the dry heat of the Imperial Valley.

It was a cultural change as well, from a diverse culture in Rochester to a predominantly Mexican-American, Spanish-speaking environment. I was changing from an academic position and migrant farm worker responsibilities to the full-time occupation of treating farm workers and their families.

I discussed this at length with Dr. Haggerty, who, realizing my dominant interest in migrant farm workers, agreed that my full-time involvement would be more effective than part-time efforts to improve conditions. He predicted that the University of Rochester School of Medicine would continue its involvement of the past five years for farm workers. Neither of us knew that the future influence of the medical school would result in two comprehensive community health clinics, in Brockport and Albion, both previous sites for migrant health clinics.

I passed the management of my pediatric clinic programs to competent directors and prepared for the move to Brawley during the summer of 1970. However, we decided to precede the move with a one-month visit to Cuernavaca, Mexico, to learn Spanish, with Alan, Susan, and Dotty sharing that visit. We flew to San Diego, where we met Dick Aronson, a University of Rochester medical student. Our first trip, with Dick driving, was a rare experience for our family. San Diego was a cool seventy degrees, but as we drove closer to the Imperial Valley, the temperature changed dramatically and the surroundings reflected the temperature, as on each side of the car we saw only bare rocks. Alan made a few comments as he checked the views.

He looked out one side of the car and remarked: "Well, I'll be damned."

He looked out the other side: "Well, I'll be damned."

He opened one window and was met by a blast of oven-hot air. He slammed it shut. When we approached the valley itself, we had a flat tire. The tire was so hot that we had to use handkerchiefs to protect our fingers.

After a brief introduction to the staff and an orientation by Dick Aronson, who was enthusiastic about the possibilities, we embarked by plane to Mexico City and then by bus to Cuernavaca. We planned to spend a month at CIDOC, a Spanish language training school in Cuernavaca. It features a Spanish-speaking faculty who allow only that language as the method of communication. Dotty, Susan, and I took advantage of the school, while Alan explored the countryside. George, our older son, was unable to leave college to join us. Our stay at Cuernavaca was a wonderful way to be together as a family, in a colorful Mexican community with a fine central *mercado,* or marketplace. We lived in a small motel complete with a spacious swimming pool, and a horse in an adjoining stall. At the end of the month, I felt confident with the rudiments of Spanish, realizing that practice later would provide more skills.

Our leave was punctuated by two events. A bull chased Alan out of a large field and almost caught him before he was able to vault to safety over a fence. Alan said he would never want to be a bullfighter following this narrow escape. When retiring during the eve of our departure, Susan was serenaded by two Mexican admirers, a fine send-off after a memorable month in Mexico.

We flew back to Rochester and packed hurriedly. We drove Alan to Wooster College and said our good-byes while en route to the Far West and new adventures. George was able to accompany Susan, Dotty, and me for the remainder of the trip.

Clinica de Salubridad de Campesinos
Brawley, California

The Clinica approached many of my ideals of community-based medicine. First, it had a board consisting of farm workers or former farm workers, and featured only one professional, a physician who practiced in the county. The president of the board was a respected, long-standing resident of Brawley. He was a careful decision maker and won the loyalty of the staff and patients alike. On a monthly basis, or more frequently if necessary, the board reviewed the progress of the Clinica. Closely associated with the board and the Clinica, Casa de Amistad, a community action program organized to fight for the rights of the Mexican-American community, was a strong presence. Its director was a seasoned community organizer, who was involved with the problems of Mexican-Americans in a society controlled by growers and wealthy landowners.

The clinic had hired a trainer for the community health workers; she was efficient and well organized, and had a clear idea of the goals of the program. She even arranged a training schedule to create an X-ray technician and a laboratory technician. Our director arranged to have a Mexican flag along one wall of the Clinica. The town of Brawley's leaders were upset and demanded that he create a flagpole for the American flag. He did this, because he wanted to cooperate with the total Brawley community in spite of his Mexican-American heritage.

I enjoyed being part of the community health clinic. I was able to have lunch at home, which was only a few blocks from the Clinica. House calls were not the habit of most of the local physicians, but were very popular with our patients. Many of the calls, usually made in the evenings, were for upper respiratory infections, skin infections, vomiting and diarrhea, ear infections, or to children with high fevers of unknown origin but requiring follow-up. Some of these fevers were due to roseola, a virus that usually resolved itself by a sudden drop in temperature on the third day, associated with a rash.

The Clinica became very popular with patients, who encountered no language difficulties and met many of the staff nurses and other personnel from similar cultural backgrounds. We were soon aware of environmental problems in the area. Frequently in Calipatria, a nearby community, I saw patients who developed sudden asthmatic attacks when planes spraying pesticides flew too close to their homes. Often these planes were guided by flag-waving young workers, who occasionally were enveloped by the sprayed pesticides. Our director complained to growers about these problems, which were never completely resolved even with his admonitions.

Brawley was a small community with one main street and a few side streets, many lined with bars. On weekends the center of Brawley was very noisy, and we usually stayed inside at these times. One weekend, one of our younger assistants was shot, not fatally, over an argument over a girlfriend. Fights were common, but usually not with guns. However, fractures were common after many of these altercations. As per the request of the workers involved with the initial planning for a grant, we did hire a bone specialist, who, as predicted, was quite busy. An internist and a pediatrician, myself, comprised the rest of the medical staff. On weekends and holidays we functioned as family physicians, as we covered for each other for emergencies.

Local physicians complained that they were losing patients because of our low-cost care. We did not refuse services to any farm worker because of insufficient funds. We believed that many of our patients could not afford the local physicians' fees, and we knew from stories told by our own board members that many patients had been refused care by these same physicians in the past.

In an attempt to protect their own medical practices, eleven Imperial County physicians sought a federal court order to prevent the proposed clinic opening on October 6, 1970. Finally, failing with the court order, two physicians filed a lawsuit against the clinic director and the president of Casa de Amistad. The farm worker community was so incensed by the new threat to survival of the clinic that they met with the board members on a weekly basis prior to the hearings in San Diego. The courtroom in San Diego on the day of the trial was packed with a standing-room-only crowd of farm workers.

Clinica de Salubridad was represented by California Rural Legal Assistance lawyers, all of whom were young and well trained and had worked diligently during the three weeks prior to the trial. The Brawley doctors had engaged a lawyer who appeared poorly prepared. The chief argument advanced against the clinic related to the statement that the doctors would lose patients to the "free socialist clinic." The lawyers for the defense countered with evidence that most of the patients could not afford private practitioners and that there was no proof that those practitioners were suffering because of the Brawley clinic. The verdict was in favor of the clinic.

Nevertheless, opposition from the local physicians continued, as reported in a *Brawley News* article on November 11, 1972:

"How much longer are the HMO freeloaders going to waste our own tax money while pretending to deliver health care to non-existent migrant farm workers. By the free clinic's own report, each doctor sees 8.2 patients per day at an average cost of fifty-two dollars per patient visit. Many of our Brawley physicians see over fifty patients a day. If they charged fifty-two dollars per visit, we would accuse them of cheating the public."

I talked to a local practitioner, who remarked, "We didn't need it; we fought it; but we got it anyway. Alone, I see twenty-five percent more patients than all three clinic physicians combined and I do it on one-tenth their budget."

To answer some of the local practitioners' complaints, I can add some personal thoughts: I sent the template for the grant applications to the Casa de Amistad, which modified it for the final application. Two Clinica physicians were board certified in internal medicine and pediatrics, respectively, while the third physician was board eligible in orthopedics. There was great reluctance of the staff of the local hospital to accept us as staff members, though we had trained in accepted programs prior to arriving in Brawley. Legally they were in no position to block us from hospital privileges even though we "practice socialized medicine," to quote one of our critics.

A Catholic nun was a factor in our eventual acceptance by the greater medical community. With a background of effective training of community health workers in another program in San Diego, she organized a similar teaching program for twelve recruits from the Brawley farm worker community. She taught basic aspects of health, including skills in taking blood pressure, pulse and respiration, patterns of breathing, and state of consciousness. She gave instructions on many of the common illnesses present in the Imperial Valley.

The sister commented: "I was impressed with the aptitude for learning that they all demonstrated, and the developing confidence in their own competence, their ability to relate to other farm worker patients in the home or clinic setting, and their enthusiasm for their work. They are performing greater than my expectations."

I would like to note one example of the effectiveness of the trained health workers: A middle-aged woman living in Brawley had developed cancer of the cervix, which metastasized to her pelvis. She needed to see specialists in San Deigo, one hundred and twenty miles away. These appointments were stressful, especially since the X-ray treatments were not helping her. Our family health workers were acquainted with her and invited one of our nurses to visit her at home. They discussed the possibilities of home care, which she welcomed. The San Diego physicians agreed that her metastatic disease was not responding and that home care under our supervision was logical.

Our family health workers visited daily, the nurse saw her two times per week, and I visited her once a week. We continued this regimen for three weeks, with more visits during her final week of life. Relatives from Mexico visited frequently. When she died at night, she was surrounded by her children and other relatives. I was present, along with a nurse and family health worker. The patient had been most appreciative of the opportunity for home care, as were her children and other family members. When the undertaker arrived, he suggested an elaborate coffin and burial ceremony. We intervened, advising a simple coffin and service for a family with limited means. Our presence made a big difference.

With our apparent competence in working with this patient, we were approached to enlarge our home care program to include the whole county, an opportunity that we accepted. This resulted in further training for our family health workers before the Clinica could be accredited by the state of California for a home care program. This was a huge step in the acceptance of the Clinica into the total medical community in a county the size of Connecticut.

Another feature of the Clinica was its frequency of making house calls. In the East I had found it an effective way to learn about a community and to establish a closer relationship with patients and families. It proved to be no different in the West, as illustrated by this example:

One evening, a family called from Calipatria, a village a few miles north of Brawley. Their child was having difficulty breathing. I visited the home, diagnosed croup, and had the mother place a teakettle on a hot plate near the child's bed so that the steam would be directed toward the child. I reassured the mother that I would remain until the child was better, with the realization that this was a frightening experience for a young mother. Even though we improvised a tent to funnel the steam over the child's bed, it was not effective in producing abatement of the barking cough. Finally, I suggested that she take the child into the shower, where a higher concentration of steam might help: It did.

During another house call, I dropped my stethoscope next to the sick child's bed, only to look at the bedsprings under the bed. I was surprised to note a dozen black widow spiders and their nests. I suggested that when the child was ambulatory, the parents should sweep out the spiders to save problems later.

At another time I noted a large bottle of Pepsi-Cola in the refrigerator. This was a favorite beverage for many families in this hot climate. I have felt that soft drinks are not a wise approach to satisfy thirst, and that the same amount of ordinary water was a better method, and not nearly as expensive. Such teaching was an important part of house calls, too.

House calls added to my understanding of families and the Mexican-American culture. I was impressed with the housekeeping of our patients in spite of the simple amenities in the home. Grandparents were living in many of the homes and cared for the grandchildren when the parents were working in the fields. In return, they enjoyed security in their older years. This was quite in contrast to many of the homes I visited in the East, where I rarely observed grandparents in the same home.

Although the Clinica was available to all of the Imperial Valley residents, it did not treat organized farm workers under Cesar Chavez. They were treated in a clinic in Calexico, on the Mexican border, about twenty miles away. I was asked to be a consultant to this program. This was a clinic sponsored by the United Farm Workers of America and was staffed by a volunteer physician, several nurses, and a few former farm workers who were trained to become community health workers. Union membership paid for the services, laboratory tests, and other benefits. There were no strikes during the time I was in the Imperial Valley (three years) but there were a number of union meetings, one of which I attended.

A striking difference between these workers and those with whom I was acquainted in the Rochester area was the enthusiasm and pride I noted in the union workers. I remember sitting among these workers during a rally for Cesar Chavez in a Calexico community building. When Cesar appeared, the clapping and shouts of "*Viva la Causa*" and "*Viva Chavez*" resounded throughout the building for many minutes.

Following one of these sessions with the union workers, Cesar sent a recruiter to visit with me at our home in Brawley. We spent several hours discussing the pros and cons of working for a union clinic that was planned in the Fresno area, in the center of the San Joaquin Valley. Though I was not ready to make a change, I agreed to visit Cesar in his office in Delano. I admired Cesar's nonviolent approach and knew that he had visited India in the past to learn in detail Gandhi's methods of organizing and nonviolence. Cesar wanted to use similar methods with union workers in California. He also realized that the field strike was not the only way to win negotiations with the growers: It must affect their pocketbooks. For this he organized grape boycotts for supermarkets in many cities in the United States, Canada, and even Europe. Prior to 1970, I had participated in boycotts in the Rochester area.

Cesar Chavez had a small office, one room, in Delano; I was impressed with floor-to-ceiling bookcases, all filled. Later I learned that his father had to sell their farm in Arizona during the Depression of 1929–30. The family joined the migrant stream and Cesar started work as a child, but only achieved a seventh-grade education before working full time in the fields. Yet, he was one of the best self-educated men whom I ever met. A visit with him convinced me that working with him would be a privilege, and I accepted.

We hired a new physician for Clinica de Salubridad de Campesinos, so that my leaving would not place a great burden on the staff. Our director's former wife was a vice president with the union; thus he understood my situation. The staff and members of the board respected my interest in the union cause, though it would break up relationships that had produced strong bonds during the past three years. Dotty and I enjoyed a colorful party and dance, with much handshaking and hugging, but believed that we would not miss the daily 100-degree temperatures of the Imperial Valley.

Volunteering with
Cesar Chavez

The next three years were to be milestones in our lives, and would challenge us as no other experience in the past. But first, I want to bring Cesar Chavez and the union goals into focus.

Born in Arizona, Cesar Chavez became a migrant farm worker as a child, when his father lost the family farm during the Depression. As full-time migrant farm workers, his family traveled throughout California for work. During this time he met Fred Ross, an organizer who had trained in part with Saul Alinski, who had helped organized the Fight efforts in Rochester, New York, in the early 1960s. Fred was director of the Community Service Organization in California. Cesar accompanied him to meetings almost daily. Fred realized that Cesar possessed unusual talents with people and hired him full time. Cesar learned that farm workers, many of whom could not read, had Social Security payments deducted from their paychecks even though nobody asked for their Social Security numbers. Later, Cesar became a director of the Community Service Organization, but resigned when the board rejected his plans to form a farm workers union.

To quote Cesar Chavez during the early days of the union: "I don't think that any one event or any one day, or any one action, or any one confrontation wins a battle. You keep that in mind and be practical about it. It's foolish then to try to gamble everything on one roll of the dice, which is what violence really gets down to. I think the practical person had a better chance of dealing with non-violence than people who tend to be dreamers or impractical. We are not non-violent because we want to save our souls. We're non-violent because we want to get some social changes for the workers."

It is with this background in farm worker organizing, and the charisma of Cesar Chavez as a leader, that we came to volunteer, with fifteen dollars per week for me and ten dollars per week for Dotty, an allowance for our apartment, and gas for the business use of our car. We moved to Sanger,

California, about twenty miles east of Fresno, in the central San Joaquin Valley. Sanger was a possible site for a future clinic, if we could find a suitable building.

The director of the program and his wife had tried for a number of weeks to locate a suitable rental for the clinic. Their lack of success was due partly to the limited budget of the union and also to the lack of suitable buildings in the adjacent communities. One evening I called a dentist who had a possible building in Kingsburg, not too far from union headquarters. It was unavailable unless we were willing to buy. "I am only interested in the money and it is purely business with me," he said.

Sharing the director's lack of success, I became aware of the criticism from Cesar Chavez, who could not understand the delays, especially when the need for a medical program was so great. I thought to myself: "Time, hopes, can we do it? Can we get our foot into at least one door? But where, when?" Among the landlords, the union was not very popular and those most sympathetic to our cause were those who owned little or no property.

One day later, I met with a physician who wanted to sell his office, not rent. He had to give up his practice because of alcoholism and drug problems. His office had adequate space and appeared to fill our needs perfectly. I continued to try to meet with him, but he would often cancel at the last minute. After many attempts, he seemed able to meet with me during the next week. This time he was so uncertain, and incapable of making up his mind or coming to any agreement, that I called off the talks.

The next day I was able to spend a few hours with Cesar at union headquarters. He outlined the struggle, the conditions of the workers, the crew boss system, and the increased wages because of union contracts. He talked of the recent involvement of the Teamsters, who signed "sweetheart agreements" with the growers but offered no real benefits for the workers. He knew the conditions of the workers, "*con simpatico*," and conveyed that feeling in a humble but convincing fashion.

Meanwhile, Francisco Tanega, a brother in the Sons of Mary, a small group of teachers and doctors, had returned from Peru, where political unrest had forced the closing of their clinic. He volunteered to join Cesar Chavez and was assigned to our project, where he was to train farm workers as community health workers for the established clinic. I discussed Francisco's planned training program for twelve or thirteen farm workers over a thirteen-week period. They were to be the cornerstone of the medical clinic when it was established. Cesar approved of this aspect of the clinic planning.

Later, Cesar had a private meeting with me and stressed the urgency of finding a temporary rental soon, even if it meant offering the owner six months' rent, "but get that office." he admonished. "We have been at this a long time and are trying, with the workers, to better their lives. The Teamsters, in contrast, are perpetuating the crew boss or labor contractor system by signing with them but not with the workers. Thus the growers hope to perpetuate the injustices of the labor contracting system, without worker involvement."

While the search for a clinic site was in progress, the *Fresno Bee* published the following report: "The first case of polio in a decade took the life of an Avenal farm worker." Cesar Chavez's office called and suspected that the death could have other causes, including pesticides. He wanted us to investigate. Francisco Tanega, Dotty, and I drove to Hanford, about forty miles west of us, to meet with the doctor who had made the diagnosis. He was a retired pathologist who maintained a microscope in his office. He told us, "You wait at my office, and I'll be there in a minute to show you the slides." These demonstrated marked nerve cell damage in the pons, deep within the brain. He commented, "I have never seen such a rapid onset in a previously healthy man or such marked nerve cell destruction with polio, but I am open to suggestions." We told him, "We plan to visit the home of the man who died," a decision he encouraged.

The deceased, according to fellow workers, was planting melon seeds with Thioran fungicide and Dieldrin insecticide, which are kept in small burlap bags. The men handled these seeds with bare hands, and the patient padded his metal tractor seat with used bags. We visited his home, which his family had left hurriedly after his death. We took samples of rice, tortillas, beans, cooking and herb oils, and pastries in case they were needed for analysis later. En route home, we stopped to talk with the doctor, who had cut more slides for analysis and was willing to assist us in any way possible. I questioned, "Would it be all right for me to forward a few slides to a doctor at UCLA Medical Center? He is a pathologist whom I had known in Rochester, but has recently moved to Los Angeles. He is especially interested in neurologic problems." He replied, "Of course. Just give me his address and I will forward the necessary specimens and slides."

Later, I studied the pathology of Thioran and Dieldrin, both of which can be readily absorbed through the skin. I learned that the brain findings were consistent with a toxin exposure rather than an infectious disease such as polio. I discussed this with the pathologist in Hanford. He appreciated our involvement. I wrote Cesar Chavez about our findings, with the hope that a definitive diagnosis might be forthcoming from the Los Angeles pathologist.

The next day, stimulated by our urgent needs, I met with a Sanger doctor, who owned a small building that appeared to have possibilities, though it was much in need of repairs. He was reluctant to rent at less than $250 per month and only with a one-year lease. "I cannot accept those terms," I countered, while visiting him in his spacious home with beautiful horses outside. During our discussion, we finally agreed on $225 per month with three-month-renewable leases. "We will do some of the necessary repairs to bring the building up to code," I offered, knowing that the union had its own carpenter available without charge to us.

Though we had reached a tentative agreement with the doctor for rental of his building, we had to wait for California State Health Department approval, which often takes a month to complete. Fortunately, I was able to arrange a visit on short notice for the state health inspector. In preparation for his visit, union lawyers asked me to obtain zoning statements, a map of the building, and a written copy of the agreement. I wanted the agreement to be signed before the doctor or Teamsters learned too much about us and our plans.

Before the agreement could be signed, we needed to install a toilet, which had been arranged by members of the Electrical Workers Union, occupants of a room in the building. I met the plumber at 8:30 AM, and he installed the toilet in two hours. When the doctor finished his office hours at 1 PM, we met him with the lease, which he signed. We believed that we could be operational in a few weeks, in time for our opening on the fifth of May (Cinco de Mayo) 1973, and in time for the first planned strike by the union in our area. Preparations included painting the interior and installing shelves that had been donated by the Valley Medical Center in Fresno.

The next few days were quite busy with other union activities, including a march in Parlier, and one in Selma, both nearby towns. In Selma one officer threatened us by driving his vehicle too close to the rear of the marchers, where a number of the women and children were frightened by the proximity of the vehicle. Only a foot away from the last marchers, I cautioned, "You are driving to endanger lives," to which he replied, "I'm only obeying orders." We were to hear this refrain too many times during the next few years.

On May 2, 1973, I left for Salinas to testify at the California Rural Legal Assistance hearings before the California Workmen's Compensation Board regarding the use of the short hoe, "El Diablo," as described by the workers. Only sixteen and a half inches long, it required workers to stoop all day while

John with short hoe—illegal in California.

thinning or weeding lettuce. Crew bosses could easily spot workers who stood to ease the strain on their backs. Those who stood too many times were dismissed from their jobs. The constant bending incapacitated many workers after a few years because of permanent changes in their vertebrae.

Growers insisted that the short hoe was the only way for proper care of the lettuce. The opposition was to present X-ray evidence and, in person, workers who exhibited inability to stand erect after years of using the short hoe. The one surgeon who was to testify for the growers did not appear because of a surgical emergency. Nine other physicians testified on behalf of the workers, included X-ray data. However, the workers themselves were the best testimony. One older worker represented the position when using the short hoe compared to the long hoe. He also demonstrated the post-working position of the back at the end of the day.

An orthopedist with whom I had worked previously in the Imperial Valley presented convincing X-rays of vertebral damage. As I prepared to testify, I stood behind a young worker getting ready to testify. She had a permanent stoop, and when standing was only four feet tall. Her X-rays showed severe vertebral damage.

Shortly after the hearings, California prohibited the use of the short hoe, a wonderful victory for the workers and their supporters. Only one state, Arizona, refused to pass legislation prohibiting its use by farm workers.

In preparation for a scheduled open house, planned for the first of May, we worked around the clock the day and night before. Equipment arrived and the staff spent most of the day arranging and storing a variety of items. At the same time, the California Department of Health nurse arrived to inspect and made some inflammatory remarks that angered our director. She also suggested that we produce a manual of how we would treat certain illnesses and emergencies, to be completed within a month. The material she requested approached the contents of a mini textbook on medicine. As the only practicing physician in the clinic, I was not going to be able to complete this time-consuming task. I cannot understand a department that should encourage improved medical care approaching its mission in such a critical fashion.

On May 5, 1973 (Cinco de Mayo), we opened at last for our open house. Amid many union flags and pictures of Cesar Chavez and other union members, and even several bouquets of flowers, we welcomed many visitors from the community and from other areas. The clinic looked spotless with its fresh coat of paint. The community health workers were most evident in their attractive blue uniforms. Punch and cookies were served and photos taken, to be published in *El Malcriado*, the union newspaper.

I had invited Dr. Lawrence Weed, author of the Problem-based Record System, to participate. This record system consisted of organized notes for each patient visit:

Subjective:	What patient tells doctor
Objective:	Results of your examination and special tests
Assessment:	Working diagnosis
Plan:	Includes treatment and future tests appropriate for the diagnosis

With this program, problems not addressed at this visit are recorded for future visits.

He suggested that we insist that all of the staff utilize the Problem-based Record System so that we could retrieve patient data with a minimum of

Open house, union clinic, Sanger. (1973)

effort at each office visit. We should use every chance to develop teaching opportunities regarding many of our patients. This would increase the effectiveness of staff members.

The first days of the clinic were busy, and somewhat disorganized. Our staff consisted of one nurse; one physician with a California medical license, and one not yet licensed in California, Francisco Tanega; a medical record librarian, Dotty; and community health workers trained by Dr. Tanega. I was unable to write complete notes immediately after seeing patients, and had to complete these after the close of the clinic in the evening. Gradually, we established our roles in the clinic, and soon functioned as a team.

A few days after the opening of the clinic, I was asked to consult at Sanger Hospital regarding a child who was thought to have encephalitis. The history revealed that the child fell facedown in the school playground, and was taken to the hospital with sand in her face and mouth. A similar fall occurred at the same time on the previous day. On examination, her eyelids were partly closed and her face was expressionless. Although she was awake, she had difficulty talking. While in medical school, I encountered similar patients in Boston, and as an intern had treated an adult with similar symptoms. I suspected myasthenia gravis, which responds favorably to a small injection of neostigmine methyl sulfate. It did, and the patient was saved from life-threatening surgery.

Myasthenia gravis is a disorder in which antibodies, called autoimmune antibodies, block receptors for a chemical messenger, acetylcholine, at the neuromuscular junction. This interferes with the nerve impulses that cause the muscle to contract. Believing this was the problem with this child, I gave a very small injection of neostigmine methyl sulfate, which, within a few minutes, resulted in a return of her muscle function, thus establishing the diagnosis. I communicated this to the physician and recommended that the child be transferred to Fresno Children's Hospital, where a long-term treatment program could be planned to assist her regular physician.

What did this accomplish for the union clinic? Word quickly circulated in Sanger that the union physician was competent, even though a volunteer.

Francisco Tanega had completed the training of our community health workers by the time the clinic opened, and they were a big help in the clinic, on house calls, and assisting patients with referrals. Frequent marches were sponsored by the union, and some of our community health workers took part. They provided a needed liaison between the clinic and the farm workers, and in one instance provided a lifesaving presence. One of our community health workers, who graduated, even though she was fluent in Spanish but much less so in English, was present when one of the farm workers was knifed in the chest. She could tell that this caused a tension pneumothorax, where air is sucked into the chest via the knife wound, building pressure that could seriously impair breathing. She found an oily rag, which she placed over the wound, causing an airtight seal. When the ambulance crew arrived, they complemented her on saving the life of the victim. She was pleased with herself, which was a tribute to her fine training under the tutelage of Dr. Tanega.

A few weeks later a young man from the American Friends Service Committee in San Francisco called and asked to visit on Saturday. Dotty and I were very tired and hoped to have a reasonably restful weekend. One more visitor added to the many we had had at our small apartment was almost too much. However, we admired the efforts of the American Friends Service Committee. A small group of Friends arrived in their bus, which was identified with a large sign, AMERICAN FRIENDS SERVICE COMMITTEE, painted on its sides. Inside they had an attractive exhibit regarding nonviolence and some information about the union. This was the first day of a planned strike by the union against a few grape growers in Dinuba, a nearby community. As with other strikes in the past, Cesar Chavez wanted to persuade the growers to sign a contract with the union.

We received permission to visit the strikers in Dinuba, and the arrival of the bus would give the strikers a morale boost, we hoped. The strikers were calling to scab workers in the field; they were recent illegal aliens from Mexico. Hired to replace the strikers, they seemed inclined to leave the fields but were frightened by the activity. Police, large, some very large, and all well armed, were stationed at the end of each row to prevent egress.

One of the growers drove by in his car, but his way was partly blocked by some of the strikers. As he edged his car into them, most of the strikers moved to avoid his bumper. A student from Stanford did not observe the car. The grower brushed his trousers with his car and would have continued had I not placed a placard over his windshield. This incensed the driver, who demanded action from the police. Visibly upset, the student told the police that they could have easily moved people away to prevent an accident. The student was so upset that I tried to stop any further confrontation with: "It won't do any good to argue, let's cool it," as I moved him away.

A few minutes later, a young worker, wearing a straw sombrero, was confronted by an officer in a menacing fashion. The officer appeared to be looking through the young man's billfold, and the young man seemed frightened at the confrontation. I moved close to him, said nothing, whereupon the officer confronted me: "Who are you?" I said nothing.

"This is a private matter," he continued, and he moved the worker three feet away. I instinctively moved closer to the harassed worker. Suddenly, I was pushed. The officer grabbed my left arm, forcibly reversed it, and twisted it behind my back. "Leave my arm alone," I said, as I felt acute pain in my arm, which had been repaired with metal plates from a fracture years previously. I was jack-knifed onto the hood of a police car and a handcuff was biting into my left wrist like the bite of a bulldog, followed by a similar bite on my right wrist.

Now I was flat on the hood of the car and someone jammed my head into the hood, knocking my glasses away. I thought to myself, *Why are they beating me up? When will someone club my head to stop this mayhem?* I gave up, collapsed, awaiting the next. I had surrendered, but no, this was not enough. Yanked off the car, I was sat upon a bar that extended along the front fender. The bar was in an appropriate position to crush my testicles, but my legs were long enough to prevent the intended trauma.

Indignity of indignities, I was thrown bodily, face-first, into the rear of the police car. Those handcuff jaws hurt. "How do you like the cuffs, really tightened them, didn't they?" came from the officer in the front seat. We seemed to be driving toward the mountains, as the road appeared to be narrower, and suddenly I felt panic. I thought to myself, *"Are they taking me to some secluded area to complete the job?"* From the officer, "A man like you should be ashamed of being on the picket lines. Why don't you work for a living?" My left hand was asleep, though I know that it could stand a loss of circulation for about an hour before there would be permanent damage.

Fortunately, we soon arrived at the Visalia jail, where I was searched and had to give up any belongings, except my wedding ring, which could not be removed because of a swollen finger. My glasses were broken and had disappeared. "Aren't you going to take off his handcuffs?" asked the admitting officer. By this time there was no feeling at all in my left hand until there was sudden warmth and tingling, followed by vibrations in the fingers of my left hand. There was a red, jagged mark all around my wrist, some blood trickling associated with swelling of the wrist and fingers.

My small cell had no windows except for a small barred one in the door, through which I could hear officers talking as they walked past. "The man must be crazy to be in the picket lines with those Mexicans." "He is a doctor, too, what makes him tick?" I was in that holding cell for an interminable time, it seemed to me, but probably three hours, before being released. I was met by a dozen people, including my wife, a lawyer, and some staff members, including three community health workers.

It was a Saturday, and I had the next day off, which Dotty and I spent working in the small garden behind our apartment. The feel of the dirt, mud on my bare feet, sharing the transplanting with Dotty, seeing the first lettuce ready for picking, was the finest of diversions. Wherever we have been located, Dotty and I found that working in a garden is a good way to relieve tension, to soften adversity, to share our feelings. It was no different with the union, except for sporadic intervals available for this relaxing aspect of our lives.

The main residual from this experience was a numb left thumb, which I learned was due to a neuroma, which would repair itself gradually. Actually, it took about a month. A criminal lawyer volunteered to take my case, which, after a year of monthly court appearances, resulted in the dropping of all charges by the police. Oh, yes, one other residual smoldered, a resentment of the power of the police, who appeared to relish their control over their victims.

Unknown persons vandalized the clinic shortly after its opening and spread yellow paint on the walls and floors, broke the front door window, and tore down the union flag from its flagpole near the entrance of the clinic. We closed for one day to repair the damage. The police were never able to find the culprits. This episode reminded us that we had many enemies, in spite of the farm worker friends who frequented the clinics.

We were becoming a team, better organized, one month after our opening day. A new nurse from Kansas and her nursing student were a welcome addition to the staff. She was well trained, with a master's degree in nursing education from Boston, and already exhibited boundless energy and ideas. I hoped that we could build the clinic around the nurse and the community health workers, with the doctor or doctors taking primary clinical responsibilities. With the Rochester program five years earlier, we had accomplished this effectively, where doctors were consultants, with the major organizational responsibilities undertaken by the nursing staff.

A former medical classmate, Dr. Ralph Merkeley, and his wife spent a day with us. He brought a Schiotz tonometer for measuring eye pressure to rule out glaucoma, numerous medical books, and, of course, his skills as a family physician. He was cordial with patients and staff alike, all of whom wanted him to return soon. He did a few months later, even though he had to drive one hundred miles from his office in Cupertino.

Another, more frequent visitor was in the person of Dr. John Blossom, director of the Family Medicine residency program at the Valley Medical Center, Fresno. He volunteered to work two afternoons a month. He was fluent in Spanish, a concerned physician, and a strong advocate for the union. He had worked with farm workers for many years, and proved a worthy associate during the years that I knew him.

On June 9, 1973, a Saturday, I was filling in for one of the union lawyers who could not attend a meeting about environmental problems for workers. It was held at the Los Angeles Hilton, where I was told that there would be a room reserved for me. There was not, and because I did not have enough money to pay, our hosts, the Los Angeles County Federation of Labor, AFL-CIO, were gracious enough to cover the costs. There were about one hundred labor leaders, and I was one of seven speakers. I spoke about the dangers of pesticides to farm workers, and said the concerted efforts of union members could improve safety conditions for all, not just union members. In the discussion, I emphasized the fact that the union provided worker committees to meet with growers about the need to cooperate on improving worker safety.

Dotty accompanied me, and the two of us relished the brief interlude from daily responsibilities with the clinic. We also talked with the former Rochester pathologist, now at UCLA School of Medicine, who, we hoped would be able to give us a definitive diagnosis regarding the worker who died of unknown causes as a tractor driver. We had investigated at the recommendation of Cesar Chavez and had the pathology slides forwarded to the pathologist at the UCLA School of Medicine.

Sunday, the day after our return from Los Angeles, I drove to Parlier, where I saw two patients and found time to attend a church service, a rare opportunity. I attended Primera Eglesia Bautista, whose congregation included many union members. The minister conducted the service in Spanish, which along with the music and flowers provided a different, necessary world in my life. Later, I took Dotty to some of these services, though there was rarely enough time for more than a few. The union felt that we didn't need time for church, since most of the staff, being Catholic, could attend early mass. Yet I felt that free time should be available on Sunday mornings, especially for community health workers with families, to share.

A new addition to the staff arrived, a physician's assistant, personable and a guitar player, who added a boost to our morale. Shortly after his arrival, we celebrated at our apartment with a sing-along, featuring the newcomer, but joined by all of us in refrain. Neighbors called the police, but by the time of his arrival, we had toned down our enthusiasm. Finding nothing to which to object, he retreated quietly, with a caution about noise. Obviously we were not the usual boisterous drinking crowd of revelers who were the cause of such complaints.

The next morning, our clinic director informed me that the union wanted only two things from me: See patients in the clinic. Recruit medical help.

In other words, don't offer suggestions. Follow orders, and forget cultivating hospital relations, teaching conferences, or outside activities except for union responsibilities. I have always appreciated dialogue and respected differing opinions, but was in a new environment where all decisions were from union headquarters. I was not the type of physician they desired, and I believed they would have readily accepted another volunteer physician to replace me. Deflated, I worked quietly for the next few days, with the realization that we were only a few months into the program, and like a colt, I needed to be broken to the regimen. Only, I was not a colt at the age of forty-eight.

On June 7, 1973, Dotty and I celebrated our twenty-sixth wedding anniversary with the determination to make the best of our circumstances and support each other as much as possible. We realized that we had to take time together whenever we could. We had little privacy with the weekly visits of younger individuals who were uncertain of their role in the union. They took over the kitchen, borrowed our car, which, on one occasion had a dislocated bumper when it was returned. "Oh, I wasn't going to tell you, since it wouldn't make much difference on that junk heap," was the response by one visitor.

I think often of our medical profession, which is trying to extract from society its "just desserts" in the form of high salaries. But why should a person, because of an opportunity for an advanced education, extract homage from thousands who are less fortunate, as in an aristocracy? Yes, we have much to learn as a society, to appreciate that we are brothers and sisters, that we have similar aspirations and similar needs for dignity and recognition as members of the same human race, whatever our origins.

Violence at the hands of the police had a profound effect on me, though I admit that I wasn't completely nonviolent at the time of my arrest. The non-violence, which Cesar espoused, has a lasting value in the struggle for justice and rights among farm workers. I accepted this, and, hopefully, this approach would smooth relations with our medical director in the future.

During the last two weeks of July, we learned that a number of farm workers were arrested on the strike lines and were in the Fresno County jail. Some were chronically ill with diabetes or had chronic infections, and we were interested in their care. We wanted to talk with the jail physician. I was never able to reach him, as he visited only one day a week and certainly not on a weekend. Furthermore, I was not allowed to visit any of the prisoners that day.

Our physician's assistant did interview several of the prisoners. A strike captain said: "I was placed in a hole, stinky blankets, no walking room, a metal bunk. In the middle of the night I was brought out of the hole for a shower. I was chased down the corridor by a policeman with a fire hose. Ten big guys with clubs beat me as I ran down the hallway."

Four other farm workers stated, "Police banged on our bars with clubs and unlocked our cells. As we came out of our cells, a fire hose was turned on us, forcing us to run along the hall where ten big officers with nightsticks, one of which broke, started to beat and scratch us."

This brutality and harassment was only the beginning of problems with the Fresno County jail, which was suddenly inundated with two hundred farm workers in August 1973. During a strike on an outlying farm, the grower obtained a court order to prohibit mass picketing around his property. When jailed, husbands and wives were in separate areas, unable to commu-nicate regarding their children, some of whom were nearby when they were arrested. Fortunately, due to our exposure of the inadequate medical care in the jail, we were allowed to have daily clinics in the jail infirmary. None of the previous violence was evident, possibly because of our presence.

A dozen Catholic priests from Fordham University in New York joined the picketers and were also arrested and jailed. They were scheduled two days later to speak at a retreat in Los Angeles, but were jailed for a week. They used this time to help build the morale of the other prisoners, who as Catholics welcomed their presence. Dorothy Day, editor of the *Catholic Worker*, was also jailed. Cesar Chavez visited her and introduced her as one of America's tireless advocates for the poor and for the farm worker.

Of these two hundred prisoners, there were a number of diabetics, one epileptic, several asthmatics, some with upper respiratory infections and hypertensives, all needing medications from our supplies. Our physician's assistant and I spent an hour or more each morning treating these various workers and their ailments. We collected messages to relatives. Outside, many supporters called for the quick release of the farm workers. The final releases were only allowed in two weeks. These two weeks gave me an opportunity to note the many flaws of the Fresno County jail and resulted in a letter to the *Fresno Bee:*

> As a physician who has observed the recent renovations of the Fresno County jail, I have the following comments. The jail has few windows and no area for outside exercise of the prisoners. Some inmates are incarcerated for a year without ever seeing daylight. There are several cages used for psychotic prisoners, and are located in a central area where they can be observed by other prisoners. These are considered central holding areas. One primitive area is the "infirmary" completely unsuitable as a medical facility. Some guards show compassion and concern for the prisoners, while others exercise pleasure in harassing inmates as if satisfying deep aggressive instincts. Sheriffs in training spend six months in this oppressive atmosphere. Most of the guards are white, and ill-trained to understand the needs of black or latino inmates. Most do not speak Spanish. The Fresno County jail needs a complete evaluation by an outside competent organization.

The sheriff-coroner offered in rebuttal that I had no competent knowledge of regulations regarding jails, or the qualifications of the medical staff, and was overstepping my expertise as a "gynecologist." "Physician, heal thyself," he concluded.

He was correct about my credentials as a gynecologist, for as a generalist, I needed more training in this highly specialized field. This was answered, in part, by the arrival of a fine nurse midwife, whose skill surpassed mine in obstetrics. We utilized the Sanger Hospital for newborn deliveries, but offered ongoing prenatal care starting in the third month of pregnancy. This included careful measurements of the size of the uterus, blood pressure, hematocrits, detailed histories of progress, and home visits when indicated. Our nurse midwife provided a supportive relationship, coupled with health education and preparation for breastfeeding.

When the patient approached term, the office visits were scheduled once weekly, always with the nurse midwife or myself. The use of the delivery room at Sanger Hospital was expensive, and whenever possible we also utilized the labor room for delivery. Our midwife was so skillful in her management of labor that all of her deliveries were considered natural childbirths without the need for episiotomies (a small incision to allow the baby's head to pass without tearing the mother's tissues).

Our nurse midwife was with the patient constantly while in labor, remained for several hours post delivery and, at the time of discharge, accompanied the patient home, where she remained for one or two days.

One of our newborns was the size of a premature infant with a weight of 4 lbs. 10 oz. She was vigorous, nursed well, and we judged her to be a small for dates infant. The mother and infant were discharged within twenty-four hours with the nurse midwife in attendance. The baby continued to nurse well.

One of newborns was born with the stomach contents outside of the abdominal wall, or gastric extrophy. We transferred the infant to Fresno Children's Hospital, where the pediatric surgeon was able to replace the stomach to its proper position without complications.

Another obstetrical problem involved a prolonged labor, necessitating a cesarean section, ably performed by the chief of surgery at Sanger Hospital with myself assisting. The mother and child were discharged, with the nurse midwife accompanying them home for the first few days of postnatal care. I learned much from our nurse midwife, whom I respected for her judgment, caring attitude, and attention to the needs of both the mothers and their babies. We were most fortunate to have her as a member of our staff.

One of the problems of utilizing volunteer physicians was the duration of their services. Cesar realized the problem and decided to send me on a recruiting tour to four major boycott cities: Chicago, Detroit, Rochester, and Boston. The union provided my airfare and one hundred dollars for spending money, with the suggestion that I stay with boycott families en route to save expenses. My first site, Chicago, netted no prospects, but in Detroit, one physician was interested and planned to visit the union headquarters to explore the possibilities. In Rochester, where I lived for thirteen years, I expected some prospects, but failed in recruiting anyone. A similar experience in Boston was most disappointing even though I had a number of contacts in that city. One of the Harvard students who had spent one summer with us at the Sanger clinic tried to help, but could not provide prospective volunteer physicians. I even had to borrow money from willing boycotters before the flight back to California.

Four cities, eight days, and one recruit. This was not an encouraging result.

The union sponsored four medical clinics, one in Delano with three physicians, our largest clinic; one in Calexico with one physician; one in Salinas with one physician; and one in Sanger with one physician—myself. Dr. Francisco Tanega took histories and was in charge of the community health workers as he was still without a California license. All of the clinics performed their own blood, urine, and bacteriology tests and were able to draw blood samples for more detailed analysis. The central medical office in La Paz bought medicines in bulk, a process that dispensed medicines at cost to patients at a considerable saving from private pharmacy charges. All of the clinics performed vision and hearing screening, electrocardiography, and development screening for children, including growth charts. Each utilized the Problem-oriented Record System as devised by Dr. Lawrence Weed. All records were kept in family folders so that all members of the family could be reviewed at the time of record audits.

The community health workers performed a valuable function. They saw many patients at home and communicated problems to the clinic staff. They were present at many field strikes and reported on conditions. They monitored the use of pesticides in the fields, and were helpful in assisting patients with referrals to hospitals or specialists. They reviewed many of their findings with Dr. Tanega, who kept a busy teaching schedule with the goal of improving their skills regularly.

Cesar Chavez believed that "house meetings" were as important as any union activity and allowed informal gatherings with patients and staff. Families would schedule an evening at one of their homes, and invite neighbors and one or more staff or union members to attend. The staff member would give a brief talk about a medical problem of interest and welcomed questions on that subject or any other subject of particular interest

Cesar Chavez (1974)

to the workers. The families could provide simple refreshments if they wished. These informal gatherings were planned for an evening every two weeks, and strengthened the bond among patients, union, and staff.

The United Farm Workers Union also scheduled marches, as for example the march on Gallo wineries in Modesto, California. The Gallo family were the largest wine producers in the United States and had never been organized by the United Farm Workers. Cesar Chavez believed that the publicity raised by a march on Gallo would result in organizing workers from Gallo for the first time. The march, scheduled in the spring of 1975, originated in communities in the central San Joaquin Valley and with sympathizers in the San Francisco area with the plan to pick up other supporters en route to Modesto, the headquarters of the Gallo brothers. The Sanger Clinic was asked to provide medical assistance, and our physician's assistant stocked medical supplies and joined with marchers from Fresno to Modesto while I met him briefly each day to review problems. A huge demonstration of union members, Cesar Chavez, supporters, and musicians gathered at the Gallo headquarters in Modesto. Joan Baez, a strong supporter of Cesar Chavez, was among the participants. It was an impressive assemblage.

Robert Chamberlin, M.D., a former colleague at University of Rochester

School of Medicine, stayed with us during the summer of 1974. He believed, with me, that the details of the union medical program should be documented. We pooled data from my experiences and his observations and together summarized the program as objectively as we understood it. It was entitled *Delivery of Primary Care—Union Style* and in brief:

The purpose is to examine one health system that has a number of unique features, in terms of the financing and delivery of care to a migrant Spanish-speaking farm population and the personnel practices developed by a consumer-controlled board of directors. This is the health program developed by the United Farm Workers of America, called the National Farm Workers Health Group. The union health plan was developed from 1969 to 1973 when the union was at its peak membership and was predicated on these statements of Cesar Chavez:

> People are healthy not because of good hospitals or good doctors or good medicine. Healthy people are a product of a healthy life. A healthy body demands that you have decent living conditions and decent working conditions. A strong contract is of much more value to the health of you and your family than a dozen clinics. Healing bodies while simultaneously healing the social ills that create conditions causing illness is truly a revolutionary and innovative approach to preventive medicine. In other words, the health plight of the farm worker is seen as a symptom of poverty and powerlessness rather than as a separate entity itself. The health plan started from the same basic premises used to develop the union. We started with two principles: First, since there wasn't any money and the job had to be done, there would have to be a lot of sacrificing; second, no matter how poor the people, they had a responsibility to help the union.

To this end, all union contracts were written so that growers agreed to contribute ten cents per working man hour into a health fund. The benefits were negotiated with the workers themselves. The most frequently selected benefits were combined into a health program and named the Robert F. Kennedy Health Program. Highest priority was given to preventive and early curative services. Benefits included pre- and postnatal care, well-child care, periodic health examinations, acute illness care, health education, and care for people with chronic illnesses. A death benefit was selected to help pay funeral costs.

Cesar Chavez (ca. 1990)

One of the key positions was that of the family health worker, who had much to do with the initial screening, interpreting for occasional non-Spanish-speaking staff members, providing health education for pregnant mothers, and being patient advocates to assist the patient to the proper agency or consultant's offices. If necessary, these workers provided care on the strike lines and visits to workers jailed for trespass. Another activity was data gathering on living conditions of workers, and on the use of pesticides in the fields by growers in order to help the union lobby for improvement in these areas.

The clinics had to rely on volunteer staff, from physicians and nurses to medical records personnel, physician's assistants, and medical and nursing students. These individuals, from a wide variety of backgrounds, needed time to become an effective team. Office hours were from 10 AM to 7 PM Tuesday through Saturday and 2 PM to 7 PM on Monday, with someone on call for emergencies at other times. Added to these hours, staff were involved in evening meetings at workers' homes twice monthly, or union meetings on evenings when urgent matters needed to be discussed.

This program provided many advantages from the viewpoint of workers, who were pleased with their care and the caring attitude of the staffs. In contrast, it placed a burden on the health workers, who tried to communicate suggestions to the central medical office, with little success. The reply was that we were not dedicated enough to the union philosophy. The complaints of no relief from the long hours, no opportunity for postgraduate education, even for a few hours, were considered not worth discussing. The union leaders were under tremendous pressure, and expected the medical staffs to withstand those stresses also. The struggle for the union to survive the Teamster encroachments had a marked effect on both the union leaders and the clinical program, and the two were intimately related. To quote from our summary: "Complete consumer control has built into it the same hazards as complete professional control, and some balance of power is necessary if the needs of both parties are to be adequately met." (It was signed Robert Chamberlin, M.D. and J. F. Radebaugh, M.D. *N.E.J.Med.*, 294: 641-645 [March 18], 1976.)

Prior to publication, we sent this to the central union office in La Paz, hoping for a response, which was not forthcoming. We realize that it may not have come to the attention of Cesar due to the many problems confronting the union at that time.

My wife, Dotty, was diagnosed with cancer of the breast in November 1974. The surgeon decided that a radical mastectomy was her best option for survival. I remember being with her when she awakened from anesthesia. Fortunately, no lymph nodes were involved and she did not need chemo or X-ray therapy. We were uncertain of the next course of action because of the high costs of the surgery and hospitalization and asked for advice from union headquarters. We were advised to apply for welfare assistance, but were rejected because the Fresno County Welfare Department could not understand that a physician would need such help. This was a serious rejection for both of us, and we realized that we must consider a change and could not pay our mounting medical bills by continuing as volunteers.

Dotty worked for a short time as medical records librarian in the clinic, but also looked for a paying job. Finally she was hired at the same hospital where she had her surgery, collecting data for a research project. This helped pay the medical bills, but slowly. I wanted to continue with the union, if possible, but realized that our future with the union was in jeopardy. This was a low point in our situation with the union, and had a considerable effect on our daughter, who was living with us at the time. Already trying to sort out her future, she did not need this worry about her mother to add to her concerns. Our two sons were also concerned, but involved enough with their own lives, one in college, and the other a cabinetmaker, to buffer their fears.

United Farm Workers march on Gallo (1975)

I remained with the union for over a year, but finally had reached a "burn-out" state, according to close friends. It was a multifaceted effect, physically, psychologically, and economically. Dotty shared in this, as did Susan. Our boys expressed relief that we planned to leave the union.

Many years previously, I had met Cesar Chavez for the first time at Cornell University, and had been in contact with him a number of times before deciding to volunteer in the medical program. I shared the same dream with Cesar, to quote him: "We must share with others who are willing to struggle until all farm workers and their families enjoy the fruits of their labor and can lead a healthy life. Those unwilling to struggle have no place in the union. Those unwilling to sacrifice so that they share their medical benefits with others have no place in our clinics. The clinic staff must not rest until health care is a reality for all farm workers and not just a hope."

I drafted a short letter to Cesar Chavez with a reluctant resignation from a program that I admired and a leader whom I respected.

On January 9, 1976, I received a letter of thanks in return, along with comments about my service over the previous three years. I treasured the letter from Cesar, whom I considered the greatest man I had ever known

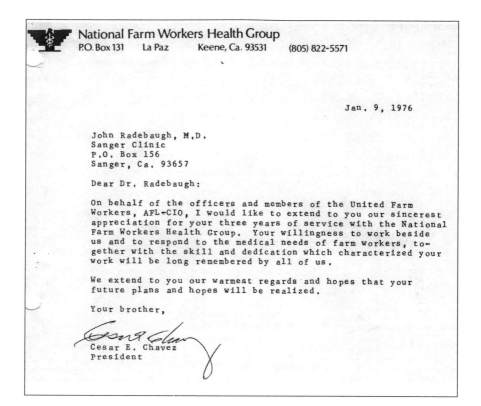

National Farm Workers Health Group
P.O. Box 131   La Paz   Keene, Ca. 93531   (805) 822-5571

Jan. 9, 1976

John Radebaugh, M.D.
Sanger Clinic
P.O. Box 156
Sanger, Ca. 93657

Dear Dr. Radebaugh:

On behalf of the officers and members of the United Farm
Workers, AFL-CIO, I would like to extend to you our sincerest
appreciation for your three years of service with the National
Farm Workers Health Group. Your willingness to work beside
us and to respond to the medical needs of farm workers, together with the skill and dedication which characterized your
work will be long remembered by all of us.

We extend to you our warmest regards and hopes that your
future plans and hopes will be realized.

Your brother,

Cesar E. Chavez
President

personally, memories that I will carry in a special place for the rest of my life. Thus ended an association that would, in retrospect, be the high point of my career.

This was a traumatic time for both of us. Dotty had been overworked, as was I, and both of us were discouraged, uncertain of our future, for we were at the lowest point of our shared careers. Yet, we had to explore options for the future, and several presented themselves. The first was with Thomas Aceto, M.D., regarding a position on the faculty at the University of South Dakota, and the second with Frederic M. Blodgett, M.D., as a director of an inner-city clinic in Milwaukee, Wisconsin. Both of these would have provided financial stability, now highly desirable for us. I chose a third opportunity, a farm worker clinic in Woodburn, Oregon, which seemed to offer stability in an interesting program.

Another physician had volunteered and was available to replace me at the Sanger Clinic, resulting in a minimal disruption of services. We said farewell to the staff, especially the family health workers, for whom I had gained a great deal of respect. Francisco Tanega was a special friend, with whom I stayed in contact for many years, but the nurse midwife, the nurse and her student, and our physician's assistant were all special people as well.

Woodburn, Oregon

After our arrival in Woodburn, in February 1976, we found a small cottage with adequate room for the three of us, Dotty, myself, and Susan and her four cats. I visited the Centro de Salubridad, a community clinic that served migrant farm workers, and some Russians who had recently settled in the area. One of the nurses was Russian, fluent in English also, and served as an interpreter for the large Russian colony. The Russians, a rural religious population, left the Vladivostok region during the Russian Revolution in 1917; moved to China, where they were not well received; then moved to Brazil, where they were unwelcome, also. The Tolstoy Foundation transferred them to Woodburn, Oregon, where they have happily settled for several years. Similar in many ways to the Amish in Pennsylvania, they kept to themselves, though the young learned English rapidly.

I was impressed with the staff and the clinic facilities, though I knew that the Department of Health, Education and Welfare office in Seattle, Washington, was the funding source. A recent letter in late January stated that funding for continuation of the clinic was not granted, and that the program would be terminated in three months. In spite of the ominous future, I remained with the program, and sought an appointment in the Department of Pediatrics at the University of Oregon teaching hospital, an attraction that appealed to my need to keep current in medical education.

I reported to the clinic and found the staff and clinic features adequate. My knowledge of Spanish was ideal for the farm worker population, but not the Russian contingent of patients. I quickly enrolled in a course in Russian at the local public school. It was a language that provided much more of a challenge than I ever encountered with Spanish. The clinic records were well kept, always important for me, and the Problem-oriented Recording System was strictly followed. The staff were competent and the equipment was fairly new and functional. We even had a laboratory technician, who was a great help to busy clinicians.

I began making house calls when indicated, easy to do in this close-knit small town. These were welcomed by housebound patients or families who did not have transportation. I continued as a clinician, aware that all of my hopes and plans might not be possible in a few months. This, of course, was not welcome news, and I knew that my training as a pediatrician was inadequate for practices that service all age groups. With adequate training, I could take the family practice boards, and if I passed, I'd be much more adaptable and competent as a generalist.

Now unemployed, and having a month available to work somewhere, I realized that it would be difficult to find employment for such a short time. I applied to some nearby farms as a farm worker and started by picking strawberries, which is back-breaking work all day long. I lasted for one week. I quickly found another job, as a cherry picker in the Hood River area, and this work was more to my liking. After two weeks, I was promoted to a "boss" because I spoke English. I was not pleased with this position, and left in two weeks.

Since I was not being paid, I arranged with the director of the clinic for a one-month leave of absence and enrolled in a course in internal medicine at Harvard Medical School, May 10–June 4, 1976, with the hope that the Woodburn Centro de Salubridad would be more stable, even re-funded, upon my return. Francisco Tanega, with whom I had worked at the union clinic in Sanger, was a Sons of Mary brother. The Mother House was located in Framingham, Massachusetts. He offered to let me board there, free for one month. I offered to play some hymns on my harmonica during their worship services. I flew to Boston and found a cordial welcome with the Sons of Mary home. It was a large, comfortable dwelling with extensive grounds of woods, fields, and hills, very close to bus and subway service to Boston.

The Sons of Mary is a missionary brotherhood that provided teachers and physicians to small programs in Venezuela and Peru, and more recently with a large orphanage in Manila, the Philippines, Francisco Tanega's home country. Originally planned for homeless "street boys," it soon accepted homeless girls. Under Francisco Tanega's direction, it offered schooling from elementary to grade twelve, with some students continuing to college.

I enjoyed the classroom environment at Harvard Medical School and absorbed new knowledge eagerly. Travel back and forth gave me an opportunity to review notes while the information was still fresh in my memory. I returned in time for the evening meal, shared with the five or six residents living there, and offered some harmonica music for the evening mass.

I returned to Woodburn with high hopes that funding for the clinics had been awarded, but these hopes were dashed. The Seattle branch of the Department of Health, Education and Welfare felt that the actions of the director of Centro de Salubridad and the domination of one family on the community board were not worthy of further funding. Fortunately, I knew the director of a program in Pueblo, Colorado, called, and learned that there was an opportunity for another physician. Unable to afford airfare to Pueblo, I asked him to provide funds, which he did.

Pueblo Neighborhood Health Centers

My exploratory visit to the Pueblo, Colorado, Neighbor Health Centers was a pleasant introduction. I was acquainted with the director, whom I had met while he was an intern at San Francisco General Hospital, and the medical director, who had worked with us one summer at the Sanger Clinic in California. Both were Harvard Medical School graduates, the medical director with a degree cum laude. Both had trained in family medicine residencies at the University of Arizona Medical School. The director had been a migrant farm worker in the past, and both were of Mexican-American background and spoke fluent Spanish. They were acquainted with the many problems of farm workers of the same ethnic backgrounds. They described the funding from the Department of Health, Education and Welfare, Washington, D.C., and this appeared adequate for their purposes.

Pueblo is the home of Colorado Fuel and Iron Co., the only steel mill between the Mississippi River and the West Coast. It was a city of 100,000 with a large farm worker, Spanish-speaking population. I visited for several days, met many members of the large staff, and appeared to meet their needs for another physician. I requested funds for the move to Pueblo and returned to Woodburn with the good news.

We moved in July 1976, anticipating a hopeful, stable future in Pueblo. A small rental home was located for us, and the staff assisted me in establishing my medical license, malpractice insurance, and other details. Fortunately, I had passed license examinations when finishing medical school, and these permitted me to practice in most states, including Colorado. I had never worked in such a large program, which featured three neighborhood clinics in Pueblo and one in Avondale, a rural community east of Pueblo. The staff consisted of two physicians, soon to be increased to three; a number of nurses, nurse practitioners, and physician's assistants; many community health workers; and secretaries. The program had close ties with the Latino community, which was represented by a Latino lawyer who would become invaluable during the next two years. There were two hospitals: St. Mary Corwin, a large general hospital, and Parkview, a smaller hospital. Both had obstetrical services.

Initially, I was actively involved with the Avondale Clinic, the smallest of our clinics. One of our earliest patients was a thirty-year-old diabetic male with vague symptoms of weakness, no pain, and an electrocardiogram that looked suspicious to me. I referred him immediately to Penrose Hospital in Colorado Springs, where, in the emergency room, he had evidence of an impending heart attack. By catheterization, he was shown to have three-vessel coronary artery disease and was subjected immediately to an angioplasty. I saw him the next day in the hospital and he seemed to be recovering without complications. I was impressed with the early onset of coronary heart disease in a young diabetic male and the threat of arteriosclerosis to even young diabetics.

At Avondale Clinic, during the following week, I saw an African-American woman with a fever and crackling noises in her chest indicating pneumonia. I took a sputum culture and gave her a shot of penicillin, with the promise that I would make a house call the next morning. At the close of clinic, I realized that she lived forty miles to the east of the clinic. I kept my promise and found her improved, and left her enough oral penicillin to complete the treatment. The round trip for this house call was eighty miles, but it was worth it.

One feature of our program bothered the local practitioners. It was the presence of physician's assistants and nurse practitioners who shared the treatment of patients almost on an equal basis with the three physicians. Of course, we were available for consultation regarding a complicated patient, and we had to countersign prescriptions. Yet, most of our patients were diagnosed and treated competently by these well-trained practitioners. Sometimes they were able to make diagnoses that we had missed, as in this example:

I was trying to find the cause of a low-grade fever in a female child, and the physician's assistant who saw her that day did a simple urinalysis to diagnose a urinary tract infection. I had not suspected it, and learned a lesson about thorough use of skills and simple lab tests to assist in diagnoses. That physician's assistant later enrolled in medical school and became a fine physician. Nevertheless, the local doctors accused us of practicing socialized medicine, and said that we were probably Communists.

Shortly after my arrival, we added another physician, bright, outspoken, who helped our staff to enjoy their free time. He and his wife enjoyed cross-country skiing and organized ski expeditions on a number of weekends, when we tented overnight. We utilized abandoned roads for these back-country tours, returning exhilarated and ready for a week of work. Dotty and I welcomed a more relaxed approach to our work than we had experienced during the past three or four years. Susan was with us only a few months before leaving to join Native Americans on the Longest Walk, from the West Coast to Washington, D.C., to meet with president Carter regarding their rights.

We scheduled weekly staff meetings on Saturday mornings, to evaluate progress, where we were encouraged to express opinions freely. During the second year of these meetings, we added the reading of *Away with All Pests*, a book by Joshua Horn, M.D., a British physician, about his involvement with the Chinese Revolution under Mao Tse-tung. Edgar Snow described it as a revolutionary book with many lessons about service for others. Dr. Horn remarked continually about "Serve the People," which was a strong message in the book. We hoped that its philosophy would improve our practices in relation to our patients.

Earlier in the history of the clinic, we three doctors wanted to improve our precarious relationship with the Pueblo County Medical Society by applying to become members. Our outspoken director had criticized the president of the Pueblo County Medical Society on several occasions. We believed that we should apply for membership to show good faith, and did so in November 1977. There was a long delay for a decision until on April 5, 1978, we received a letter that we had been "rejected by vote of the membership." Our medical director felt that this should not be accepted without contesting it. He wrote to the Colorado State Medical Society and requested a full review of the circumstances that led to our rejection. Again there was a long delay, until on January 25, 26, 27, 1980, the Judicial Council of the Colorado State Medical Society held hearings in Pueblo.

During the hearings, we presented much background material, including letters of recommendation from physicians whom we had known in the past. After long deliberation, the Judicial Council sent two of us doctors letters that we were acceptable, but refused the application of our physician-director. With this news, in support of our director, we both withdrew our applications for membership in the Pueblo County Medical Society. The three of us never applied again to that group.

In 1977–78, our staff increased considerably. We employed five doctors, seventeen nurse practitioners or physician's assistants, and a dozen community health workers. With a staff numbering seventy, we offered a complete program of care for patients, including obstetrics, minor surgery, some dental care, house calls when indicated, and hospital care. We readily referred patients in need of surgical care, but treated medical and pediatric patients in both of the Pueblo hospitals. When necessary, we had a series of consultants for those patients needing intensive care or specialized procedures.

Occasionally, we had speakers from other parts of the country for teaching sessions at the Pueblo Neighborhood Health Centers. Dr. Allan Butler, retired chairman of the Department of Pediatrics at Massachusetts General Hospital, was our first visiting professor, on October 20, 1977. I introduced him as a long-standing advocate for improved medical care. Since his retirement in 1960, he was a prime mover in establishing a prepaid medical program for the United Auto Workers Union in Detroit. He helped start the National Head Start Program to educate children of poor families in the years before kindergarten. He advised: "We must introduce an incentive to keep people well rather than the present archaic fee-for-service system. Furthermore, well-trained nurse practitioners and health associates can deliver a people-oriented service to help the busy solo practitioner who is often unable to spend enough time with patients."

During the week that Dr. Butler visited us, he observed each of the clinics and talked with many of the staff doctors, physician's assistants, nurse practitioners, nurses, and family health workers. He wanted us to make peace with the local medical society and to pursue strong ties already established with some of the local physicians. He wanted to see more participation of all of the staff in meetings and more involvement of community health workers in actual patient care. He approved our reading of *Away with All Pests* by Dr. Joshua Horn as being a fine stimulus for all of our staff.

I was surprised and pleased that he returned his honorarium to be utilized for Pueblo Neighborhood Health Center programs. As I look back on his visit, I realize what an inspiration it was to have such a perceptive warrior and teacher with us.

On March 24–25, 1978, our next visiting professor was Dr. Victor Sidel, chairperson and professor of social medicine at Albert Einstein College of Medicine, New York. Long active in Physicians for Social Responsibility and

International Physicians to Prevent Nuclear War, the latter receiving the Nobel Peace prize in 1985, he was an outstanding advocate for nuclear abolition. He visited China in 1971, 1972, and 1977, and his wife, a psychiatric social worker, accompanied him. She published *Urban Survival, The World of Working-Class Women,* and coauthored with her husband *Serve the People,* or *Observations on Medical Practices in China Today.*

They both initiated a lively discussion comparing traditional Western practices and those in China. They were familiar with *Away with All Pests* and endorsed its message of "Serve the People." They seemed impressed with the neighborhood health centers and staff, and our caring attitudes about patients, and encouraged us in our efforts. Again we were fortunate to have such outstanding teachers, even for only a few days.

Several experiences are worthy of further comment:

A young woman appeared with right lower quadrant abdominal pain while I was on emergency duty at Parkview Hospital. My examination revealed tenderness of the type associated with appendicitis, but the patient had missed her last menses, making me suspect a tubal pregnancy. I called an obstetrician, who did not examine her but felt that he could see her in the morning. In a quandary, and not wishing to cause problems, I weighed the risks. I called another obstetrician and told him that I was concerned that this was an ectopic pregnancy. He examined her and agreed, then operated to find an ectopic pregnancy, from which she recovered without incident. I had always been taught to investigate suspected ectopics (tubal pregnancies in the fallopian tube) as an emergency as it could rupture and bleed profusely at any time.

The second experience was one I did not believe would ever happen to me. I was called to make a visit on a woman whom I had treated at home for pneumonia one year ago. She had never been a regular patient in any of our clinics. An obese woman, she complained of lower back pain and did have tenderness of her lower spine. She was unable to get out of bed because of the pain. I gave her a prescription for Tylenol (similar to aspirin), and told her that one of our nurse practitioners would make a follow-up call the next day. On the following day she appeared unchanged. Two days later, she appeared stuporous, and the nurse practitioner referred her to the emergency room at St. Mary Corwin Hospital. The doctor on duty noted that she had undergone orthopedic surgery for one of her knees two weeks previously and called the surgeon, who ordered that she be admitted; he would see her in the morning.

The next morning she was again stuporous, and now febrile, and he asked for an internal medicine consultation. The consultant noted a rigid neck and performed a spinal tap, which revealed meningitis. She was immediately treated successfully over the next ten days. The origin was a staphylococcus, the cause of which was considered an infection from the knee surgery with secondary spread via the bloodstream to the meninges. She was persuaded to sue, which she did, charging me, the other doctors on our staff, the nurse practitioner involved, the emergency room physician, and the hospital with malpractice. The orthopedic surgeon was not implicated.

If I had seen the patient in follow-up myself, would it have been different? I don't know, for meningitis due to staphylococcus may develop more slowly than in the acute progression associated with hemophilus, pneumococcus, and meningococcus, the more common causes of meningitis. As a pediatrician, I had seen many of the latter types in practice and should not have missed meningitis, even in an adult. Yet I was devastated, for it was the first and only time I have ever been sued, and I had no confidence in the outcome.

The malpractice trial took several years, in which the hospital, our nurse practitioner, the emergency room physician, and our two health center physicians negotiated a settlement through their lawyers. I did not settle, for I felt that the patient had no symptoms or signs of meningitis when I first visited her, four days prior to being admitted to the hospital. I reviewed the literature of staphylococcus meningitis and found that it could be insidious in onset, making it difficult to diagnose. Long after I left the Pueblo Neighborhood Health Center, I received a letter from my malpractice lawyer, stating that on January 6, 1986, a copy of the Order of Dismissal without Prejudice for failure to prosecute (i.e.: the plaintiff did not appear) was issued. What a relief, for a situation which deflates and humbles a physician completely. Fortunately, the patient recovered without sequelae.

A greater problem surprised us all at the Pueblo Neighborhood Health Centers on April 15, 1978, at one o'clock in the afternoon. The district attorney had received a search warrant to enter the Pueblo administrative offices. Two women from the program refused, and telephoned for help. A deputy district attorney thereupon gained entry by breaking a window, allowing his staff and police to enter, confiscate, and copy medical records supportive of Medicaid claims that had been filed by the center. They continued this until ten at night on April 15, and continued from eight in the morning to three in the afternoon on April 16. At the same time, they impounded all of the clinics records for twenty-four hours. It was unknown how many records were copied. In addition, they confiscated a copy of *Away with All Pests*, found on one of the secretary's desks.

The next day the following headlines appeared in Denver newspaper:

"PUEBLO DISTRICT ATTORNEY BREAKS INTO DEN OF MAOISTS" (this directly related to the book *Away with All Pests*, by Dr. Joshua Horn, M.D., who worked with Mao Tse-tung and often quoted his motto, "Serve the People") —April 16, 1978.

"District Attorney Accuses Neighborhood Health Center of Medicaid Fraud."

The above events caused havoc among many of our patients and our staff, for we were unable to function for about forty-eight hours. Many of our patients were incensed enough to meet together with a lawyer for the clinic, and decided to attempt to recall the district attorney, who had been involved in other scandals. The investigation, assisted by the Office of Program Integrity regional office, continued for many months, and the allegations were proved wrong. In addition, the district attorney was recalled in direct relation to the strong community opposition to his methods.

During the turmoil surrounding the break-in by the Pueblo district attorney, I made many house calls on older patients, especially those who had no transportation, to reassure them that we planned to continue our services and that emergency coverage would still be available. I observed that the Neighborhood Health Clinics never recovered from the bad publicity engendered by the break-in, for it produced some conflict within the administration and the board, which I will try to explain.

Our administrator had made some important decisions without consulting the board. His position as director of the clinics and as a practicing clinician made it difficult to delegate responsibility, a weakness of the position. The situation was troubling to me, for I did not want to be part of the undemocratic approach to managing our clinics, nor to be involved in offering less than optimum care for our patients. I was proud of our concept of open clinics that did not turn away anyone regardless of economic status, race, or religion, and tried to treat patients equally and with care. For the time being, the best thing for me was to continue humbly with my primary responsibility, the care of patients.

To add to our problems, several of our physicians considered leaving, including a fine pediatrician and a superb generalist, the latter an outspoken critic of our director. Eventually they both resigned, a real loss to the program. Patients, too, were upset, and I tried to listen to their concerns and pass them on to the administration. During the latter months of 1979, relations between the director of administration and the staff deteriorated. Board intervention was sought but not forthcoming. Finally, some staff members, including myself, decided to confront our director with a petition, signed by fourteen members of the staff to form an employees union. This was met with dismissal by our director, without comment. Meanwhile, relations between the director and the medical director became intolerable. Both had been close friends from medical school and residency days, but present differences resulted in the resignation of the medical director, a brilliant clinician who was fair and just with the rest of the staff.

I felt that my future with the Pueblo Neighborhood Health Centers was in jeopardy. I explored possible positions but wanted to remain working with farm workers. One of the possibilities was the Sunrise Health Center, Greeley, Colorado, in the northeastern part of Colorado. I visited, liked the director, and saw an opportunity to develop a warm and caring program near Greeley Hospital, with its excellent family practice residency. By this time, I had passed the family medicine boards, which gave me credentials in family practice to add to credentials in pediatrics, thus helping me to be more adaptable for a variety of primary care positions. I met with the board, staff, and director and presented my credentials. I felt comfortable with the members of the program, and they with me.

Sunrise Health Center, Greeley, Colorado

*I*n July 1980, we prepared to leave Pueblo, after two years of optimism and satisfaction and one year of problems with the district attorney and management. Finally, we learned that there was no Medicaid fraud and that the break-ins were an unnecessary publicity maneuver by the district attorney. It was difficult to say good-bye to most of the staff, many of whom were outstanding with their services. The community health workers were essential members of the program, and one of them was an effective mediator between the administration and the staff. Not only did we have many friends in the staff, but we had warm friendships with several neighbors as well, two of whom Dotty corresponded with for many years.

Greeley, Colorado, is located in the north-central region of the state and has about half the population of Pueblo. To the east are flatlands and to the west are the foothills of the Rocky Mountains. It is an area of stockyards, which permeate the atmosphere with a distinctive odor. Many vegetable farms are also in the region, and these employ a number of migrant farm workers. The clinic itself has one small building, with a staff of ten, in contrast to the seventy in Pueblo. The director spoke Spanish fluently and had a business background. His demeanor suggested both efficiency and fairness.

As the medical director, I was expected to develop a cohesive staff and a teaching program beneficial to all of the staff. I was expected to develop a cooperative relationship with the Greeley Hospital and medical society. I met with the visiting nurses to learn of the greatest needs from their viewpoint. I approached the clinic staff by listening to understand the problems as they visualized them.

The community board hired me for a one-year term, with continuation yearly at the discretion of the board and the director. Benefits were clearly outlined, including malpractice insurance, health insurance, medical society dues, one week of postgraduate training, and a short vacation period. This was the clearest agreement that I had ever negotiated, and it provided the kind of security to which I was unaccustomed in previous programs.

Upon arrival, I found that the clinic was in the process of reconstruction, allowing more space for patient examinations and more room for medical record storage. It featured a central nurses station so that patients could be moved from room to room more expeditiously. The windows were such that the clinic was bright, and in summer had good ventilation. The director was in direct communication with me and the rest of the staff so that changes could be enacted without delay. Thus, my first year started in optimistic fashion.

One of our earlier patients was a one-year-old child who was not growing, had a distended abdomen, and passed recurrent foul-smelling diarrhea. He appeared emaciated, almost like a child with celiac syndrome, a chronic inherited intestinal disease related to a sensitivity to wheat gluten. Another possibility was an infection with *Giardia lamblia*, a parasite found in infected water or in day care nurseries where the organism is easily passed from child to child. I made a few house calls to obtain fresh stools from the child and took them to the Weld County Hospital bacteriology laboratory, where the diagnosis was confirmed. Over a period of time, treatment with a specific antiparasitic medicine was effective in curing the child.

I recall teaching rounds at Penrose Hospital, Colorado Springs, when one of the pathologists showed electron microscope photos of small intestinal biopsies of this condition. The tiny parasites were lined up like pigs at a trough so that there was no area of the intestine available for the absorption of nutrients. This explained the malnutrition in these patients. Fortunately, I had a few slides to show at a teaching session at our clinic.

House calls, which were possible within twenty-five miles of our clinic and most within the environs of Greeley, proved to be useful. I am reminded of one in particular relating to a woman who lived ten miles out of town. She had an acute asthma attack and I gave her a small shot of epinephrine to relieve the symptoms. Her house was surrounded by hay fields and I wondered whether she was allergic to the hay itself. She had no transportation, so I was not able to refer her to an allergist for skin testing.

Generally, I made fewer house calls in Greeley than in some former locations, though I found them easier to complete because of the smaller size of the town. I usually made them in the afternoon after office hours. I saw one young woman with a generalized rash, no fever or sore throat. I suspected rubella (German measles) and drew a blood sample with a high rubella titer of 1:320, which promptly dropped to 1:10 when the rash disappeared. Fortunately, she was not pregnant, for this is a serious cause of fetal abnormalities during pregnancy. Over a Labor Day holiday, I made six house calls, one of which resulted in a hospital admission. One patient, knowing that house call bills double that of an office visit, opted for an office visit, which I obliged.

The Sunrise Clinic included an active dental program, unusual in many community health programs but equally as important as a medical program. We featured a well-trained nutritionist, who was especially effective with our diabetic teaching. Our active outreach program offered a number of services in the homes, and we developed a weekly Spanish class for those of our staff who were not Spanish-speaking.

There were problems with me, as the schedule consisted of seeing patients every fifteen minutes, with thirty minutes allotted for complicated patients. I did not adjust to this schedule very well and came under frequent criticism from the nursing staff for delays. Although half of our patients were walk-ins—without appointments—causing disruptions in scheduling, they were less disruptive than I with less than optimum compliance with the tight timetable. One morning, on the way to work, I saw one of our patients with difficulty maneuvering his wheelchair across nearby railroad tracks, stopped to help, and drove him to the clinic. I saw him first, thus backing up the clinic for the rest of the morning, inexcusable.

There were other problems with me, such as poorly planned reports to the community board and equally inadequate weekly meetings for the medical staff. I was successful, however, in creating cordial relations with Weld County Hospital, with the result that family practice residents occasionally helped us in our clinics. Most of our hospital patients were cared for by specialists, as with one of our patients, a child with a fractured femur. I took a monkey hand puppet to entertain him, and a few days later I saw several other hospitalized children with a similar monkey.

At the end of my first year with the program, Dotty and I took our vacation by camping in the Snowy Mountains of Wyoming for one week. It was a wonderful vacation, away from crowds, no telephones, and we returned well rested and ready for the coming weeks. I was surprised to have a notice from our director to meet him in his office; he dismissed me for the following reasons:

Less than adequate adherence to the appointment schedule for patients.

Less than adequate preparation for weekly staff conferences and for board meetings.

I was not pleased, but realized that he had sufficient reasons for the dismissal. This change was not expected and resulted in a quandary about what to do next. Dotty was equally disappointed about having to move only after one year in Greeley. She liked the community, saw me much more than in previous programs, and enjoyed the proximity to the Rocky Mountains. In desperation, I called the former medical director of the Pueblo Neighborhood Health Centers, who was the new medical director of the Alviso Community Health Center in San Jose, California. He mentioned that if I were to consider joining him, I "would be jumping from the frying pan into the fire." He would welcome me if I decided to come, which I did. We were able to sell our home without problems, and hired a moving van, while we drove our two well-used cars across the salt flats, through Nevada, and over the mountains to San Jose, tired but hopeful for a brighter future with Alviso.

Alviso and Stanford Programs

We moved in August 1981 to Mountain View, California, midway between Palo Alto and San Jose. This urban setting was with the Alviso program, which had problems similar to ones we had already encountered. There were many farm workers, and ghetto conditions for many multilingual patients, such as Mexican-Americans, Vietnamese, and Chinese, and lesser numbers of a variety of cultures, including some from Afghanistan, Hmong from Cambodia, and Laotians. The Alviso program was larger than the Pueblo Neighborhood Health Centers, with three busy clinics. The program had ties with Stanford Medical School. We employed seven full-time physicians and a number of part-time doctors, the latter working one afternoon a week at the Alviso Clinic.

The program was federally funded under the Health, Education and Welfare Department and featured a director who was responsible to a board of farm workers, one local physician, and representatives from the Vietnamese and Chinese communities. The medical director was a talented family physician whom I respected from previous associations at the Pueblo Neighborhood Health Centers. We shared similar ideas about primary health care even though I was just recovering from a failure in Greeley.

Some of the problems that I was warned about became evident after the first few staff meetings. Records were often misfiled and not available at the time of a patient's appointment. Many patients with transportation problems were late or unable to keep appointments. Some of the part-time physicians were late for their scheduled clinic times and left early to attend to problems with their private offices.

Every new setting has lessons to be learned. For example, I stopped at the Olinder Clinic to sign a few records on a rainy day, perhaps no longer than fifteen minutes. When I returned to my car, I found that the passenger seat was soaking wet and the window broken. My radio was missing. I suspect that someone in a nearby apartment saw me leave and made an easy acquisition. On another occasion, after leaving the McKinley Clinic late in the evening, I parked my car in the shed behind our apartment and crawled into bed. I heard a banging noise outside, but fell asleep, exhausted. In the morning I found my driver door jimmied and my medical bag missing. Obviously, someone had followed me home, in a search for drugs, none of which was in my bag. I never left my bag in the car again.

The visiting nurses, soon aware that I made house calls, referred patients whose doctors refused to visit them at home or who abandoned them when they were transferred to nursing homes. Some were referred because they had been abandoned for nonpayment of medical bills. These were all welcomed into our program.

One of the first such referrals was A.C., a sixty-five-year-old woman with advanced rheumatoid arthritis who was bedridden in a second floor apartment. She had no insurance and a husband who drank heavily. I had no time for a full evaluation, but planned to come back in several days. After reviewing her hospital records, I returned to complete the evaluation. I arranged for visiting nurses and physiotherapists to visit her twice weekly.

During the next year, she improved gradually and was able to use a wheelchair and finally crutches. I obtained disability benefits for her, and after long, persuasive attempts with the landlord influenced a move to a first-floor apartment. Unable to affect her husband's drinking, I finally arranged admission to the Veterans Administration hospital for alcoholism. After eighteen visits in two years, I decreased her medications to aspirin in tolerated doses. Psychologically, this woman was much more optimistic about her course. A complete home care program was necessary for her, as there was no way for her to come into the clinic.

Another home patient was a sixty-year-old woman with cancer of the ovary and liver metastases, in considerable pain. Her pain could not be managed successfully, and she was transferred to Hospice for around-the-clock care.

A thirty-four-year-old woman with a drug-abuse problem and hepatitis lived in extreme poverty and had very little food for her two children. I arranged for surplus food and visiting nurse assistance.

A ninety-two-year-old man was recovering from a stroke and had three falls from slippery floor rugs, but his supportive family preferred home treatment. I arranged to have the rugs replaced, and made four other house calls during the next four weeks. He was considerably better with additional help from the visiting nurses.

I visited a three-year-old child recovering from chicken pox, complicated by scarlet fever and an ear infection. Scarlet fever is caused by a streptococcus bacterium and responded to a long-acting shot of penicillin. When I saw him ten days later, he was recovered.

These are but a few examples of the variety of patients seen on house calls, always unpredictable but often rewarding. They add to the flexibility of a medical practice and usually provide more information about a patient than can be gained by many office visits. Patients who have no transportation or are bedridden are grateful for the extra convenience to them.

It is important for physicians to keep abreast of medical progress, and I usually accomplished this by attending grand rounds at San Jose Hospital or the Valley Medical Center, both in San Jose. I have always gained from these rounds wherever I am located because many of the points made have immediate value for a general medical practice.

One of the difficulties with the Alviso program was long waiting times for some patients. These were frequently the result of slow retrieval of misfiled records. Sometimes they were related to late arrivals of physicians, especially the part-time doctors. Many of them compounded problems by leaving before they had seen all of their scheduled patients, claiming that there were urgent matters to attend to at their offices. Though we full-time physicians complained about this, little was done to correct the problem.

The board decided that the director needed to be dismissed, but did not have a replacement. They advertised for many months before a suitable candidate responded, none other than the former director of Clinica de Salubridad, in Brawley, California. On his first day in office, wanting to start with a clean slate, he dismissed the medical director without warning and called me into his office. He commented, "John, I see that you are up to your usual political activities; you're fired."

Fortunately, both the former medical director and I had local employment options and received faculty appointments at Stanford Medical School. I was offered an associate clinical professorship in the Department of Community and Family Medicine at Stanford, and was asked to teach part-time with the family practice residency at San Jose Hospital. These positions helped to buffer the shock of leaving the Alviso program. In addition, our apartment in Mountain View was conveniently located midway between the

Stanford campus and San Jose Hospital, so moving our living quarters was not necessary.

The director of the Division of Community and Family Medicine was Dr. Count Gibson, who had gained nationwide fame for developing an African-American community medicine program in Mississippi, a model for similar programs in the United States. More recently, he had developed a clinic for farm workers in Livingston, about fifty miles east of Palo Alto in the San Joaquin Valley.

I was placed in charge of the preceptor program for Stanford's first-year medical students. In preparation for spending two months with a family practice preceptor, I developed a didactic teaching program for first-year students. I taught the importance of caring, of learning to listen to patients, and of not being hasty with advice. I tried to emphasize promptness with appointments with the doctors, and the value of telephoning the preceptor if unable to attend because of sickness or any other reason. I had learned this the hard way in Greeley, Colorado. I taught the simple courtesy of addressing patients as Mr., Mrs., or Miss with the last name; never to use nicknames; and to address by a first name only if the patient insisted.

The majority of preceptors, who were my age or younger, were eager to have students and share thoughts with me. I planned to visit each preceptor at least once during the student rotation and found this an easy process, since most of the preceptors were located within a short distance of Stanford. Though some were twenty-five or thirty miles away, this was not a problem for most students. All of the students were in their first year and soaked up information like sponges. They were pleased to have an opportunity to work with live patients, and to correlate their illnesses with some of their didactic teaching. In the experience of many preceptors and faculty, students retained the knowledge gained from patients as a fine adjunct for textbook learning.

While teaching at the San Jose Hospital Family Practice Residency, I tried to encourage home visiting, teaching by example. Also, I made a few mistakes, illustrated by the following:

One night, I was on call for the residency practice at San Jose Hospital, and was asked by the house staff to supervise a delivery. This was uncomplicated, and they delivered a lusty, active term male infant. Reassured that all was well, I decided to return home when, unknown to me, the residents had difficulty delivering the placenta. Eventually the residents delivered the placenta without complications, though I should have been present to assist. The next day the chief of obstetrics, upset at my lack of action, criticized me severely. I had no excuses, for I should have remained until the placenta was passed.

The following examples illustrate the infinite variety of house calls. I planned to see a post-cesarean section patient two days after hospitalization to check on her abdominal wound and to advise her about nursing, if indicated. I felt that a mother should try nursing for the antibodies that the baby receives from her milk and for bonding with her baby. All was well, and I arranged for visiting nurse follow-up in a few days.

A thirty-year-old woman with hyperemesis (vomiting) in early pregnancy lived in a meager home with an unsupportive husband. Since she had a history of alcohol excess, which placed her in a high-risk pregnancy, I referred her to an obstetrician. I would follow up later to check on her progress.

A seven-month-old child presented with a three-day fever to 105 degrees intermittently and a supple neck. Following a quick exam, I reassured the mother. I called in the morning, when the child was afebrile with a mild generalized rash. Diagnosis: roseola, a viral illness, with a benign convalescence.

I saw an eighty-one-year-old woman with a TIA (transient ischemic attack) at two in the morning. I sent her immediately to the hospital for admission, for carotid sonogram and anticoagulant therapy because of possible impending stroke.

An eighty-eight-year-old woman with a history of four heart attacks and congestive heart failure was treated at home. I made a series of four follow-up calls that I shared with visiting nurse calls, until her condition deteriorated and I transferred her to a convalescent home for further care.

An unusual patient was a fifty-four-year-old woman with scleroderma, an uncommon disease with muscle pain and stiff joints, similar to rheumatoid arthritis. She also had chronic renal disease, skin hardening, and esophagitis, often associated with this disease. She was so sick that I admitted her to the hospital for intensive therapy and consultation with a rheumatologist. Eventually she was discharged for home care. During the next two years, I treated her with frequent visits at home with the help of visiting nurses and physiotherapists. She was hospitalized again a year later, followed by more home care. Finally she needed full-time hospice care because of the gradual progression of her incurable disease. Even this patient, who suffered from scleroderma since age eighteen, was amenable to home care and was happier in that environment than anywhere else.

Occasionally a house call uncovers a surprise that can be solved only by a diligent effort, well beyond the usual parameters of medical practice. The visiting nurses referred a family who lived just south of the San Jose city line in a semirural area. I had difficulty finding the small home, which was surrounded by high raspberry bushes with only a dirt road leading to it. I met a middle-aged woman who had just received a notice from the welfare department saying that her welfare benefits were canceled and that she should find full-time work immediately. She was distraught, for she was the only support for three retarded children, all in their twenties, who though ambulatory could not support themselves. They would have to be moved into an institution! She said she would commit suicide before allowing that to happen.

I assured her that I would do all I could to help. I promised to try to persuade the welfare department not to drop her from the rolls. Hoping that this would not be an idle promise, I immediately met with the visiting nurses to plan our action. We calculated that the cost of three retarded children in an institution would cost the county far more than continuing the present support, thus allowing the mother to care for her three children as she had been doing for so many years.

I suspected that some official made this arbitrary decision without knowing the details, and was contributing more tragedy to an already unhappy situation. A few more house calls were in order, and a court appearance was necessary to resolve the dilemma. The mother and her three offspring, a visiting nurse representative, a social worker, welfare department representatives, and I were present. Our arguments were convincing enough to persuade the judge to issue an order to continue the present support of this mother. I was most pleased with the outcome of this unusual situation, a problem considered to be out of the realm of medicine. To my mind, it is fully as important as the common practice of overlooking the social problems that often complicate medical care.

One of our patients in the Family Practice Clinic at San Jose Hospital was an older Japanese woman, always neatly dressed, who visited for control of her hypertension. I knew that she lived in a high-rise senior-citizen complex and decided to visit her at home, feeling that her trips to the clinic were an unnecessary effort. When I visited her apartment, I was pleased to see an immaculate, well-kept space, with some beautiful Japanese furniture and a large woven Japanese tiger wall hanging, which had been in her family for many generations. Her blood pressure approached normality in her own home. I left with considerable respect for this very self-sufficient woman, the epitome of aging with dignity.

I visited an Italian woman with bronchitis in the same senior-citizen complex. I was equally pleased by the contents of her apartment. She had accumulated an international doll collection, mostly European, sent by her many relatives during their travels. My understanding of this woman and of the previous patient was enhanced by these house calls.

I saw a Vietnamese child for otitis media in the office, and told the family that I would visit within a week for follow-up. Much to my surprise, there was no furniture in their tiny apartment and very little food in the refrigerator, although the child's otitis was much better. I quickly applied to several aid programs for help. Many Vietnamese families, "boat people," had arrived as refugees after having undergone many risks and lost all personal belongings in their struggles for survival.

Southeast Asians were often crowded into small apartments, several families in a space large enough for only one family. I was impressed by the care these families took to provide help for relatives and friends to become established in a foreign environment and culture. What stories many of these people could tell about their sacrifices and struggles!

I divided my time between the Community Medicine Department at Stanford and the family practice residency at San Jose Hospital. One afternoon, while driving on the expressway from Palo Alto to San Jose, I noted that the wind seemed to make my car difficult to control for a few minutes. Upon arrival at the clinic building, I found all of the staff standing around it, looking up at the top.

"We just had an earthquake!"

"It knocked down all of the books in the bookcase!"

"I felt seasick with the swaying."

"We were ordered to leave the building immediately."

"The building is being inspected to see whether it is safe for us to return." Obviously the control difficulties I noted with my car were caused by the earthquake.

Leona McGann was my immediate supervisor at Stanford. She was a medical social worker with additional training in public health. A warm supportive family medicine advocate, she was the major cause of Stanford's vitality in that subject. As part of the program, she developed student visits to unusual rural programs, often culminating in an overnight stay at her cottage in the mountains near Yosemite National Park.

One of these rural visits was to the Livingston Clinic, in the northern San Joaquin farming area. After seeing the clinic in action, our entourage had supper of barbecued chicken, salad, and pie and ice cream at the home of one of the clinic board members. Following this we had a discussion with board members. The Livingston Clinic treated a variety of patients, some with medical insurance, many more without. Most of the patients were farm workers. After staying at homes of many board members for the night, the students were treated to a hearty breakfast of pancakes, eggs, and peaches, with plenty of refills, at the home of a local grower, "Sweet Potato Joe." Heading for the mountains, we climbed beautiful rolling hills, stopping at noon at a Buddhist monastery, complete with well-manicured vegetable gardens, a large bell to summon people to meetings, and a small retreat, which housed a leader and two monks. The older Buddhist leader conducted meditations for students, who were impressed with his knowledge, succinct advice, and open approach to questions. We adjourned to a nearby clinic, staffed by two family practitioners, who were both Buddhists. They kept superb records, seemed to welcome patients as partners in their care and treatment programs, and used very few medicines, but nevertheless seemed to meet the needs of their patients, Buddhist and non-Buddhist alike.

Our entourage climbed farther into the hills to rendezvous at Leona McGann's simple cottage, which enjoyed a spectacular view of the mountains and hills to the east. Some of us slept in tents, while others availed themselves of the cottage accommodations. We enjoyed a barbecue planned by the students, followed by a meeting in which we commented about our impressions of the past twenty-four hours. It was immediately evident that there were lessons for all of us, practically and spiritually, adding to understanding of varieties of methods to accomplish the same goals.

The assistant dean for minority studies at Stanford was particularly interested in a Native American medical student, L.C., a Navajo, a graduate of Dartmouth College. The assistant dean, also a Native American, was a warm hostess and opened her apartment to minority students at Stanford and offered strong support for them.

The Zuni reservation in New Mexico asked for her assistance and she sent me to explore the possibilities of a teaching association. The Zuni Pueblo encompasses 407,000 acres with a population of 7,754, almost a third below age sixteen. It has a fine small general hospital, and its physicians are engaged in a unique preventive program for diabetics, who represent twenty-five percent of the population over forty-five years of age. Famous runners in the past, they have become overweight through lack of exercise and a diet high in carbohydrates.

The program featured exercise classes twice weekly and aerobic and strength training, along with nutritional teaching and close monitoring of weight and blood pressure. Most participants averaged half a pound to one pound of weight loss per week and gradual lowering of blood sugar over the first few years.

One of the young women who greeted me at the hospital was a graduate of this program and informed me that her diabetes was now easily controlled. Hospital staff and the tribal board were interested in a program involving Stanford Medical students for at least a two-month rotation cycle.

The assistant dean was invited by a member of the Aberdeen, South Dakota, headquarters of the Indian Health Service to visit their facilities, and she accepted. She wanted L.C., our Navajo student, and me to accompany her. We flew to Rapid City, South Dakota, where we were introduced to the many problems in that area and in Pine Ridge, both in the extreme western part of the state. We visited the hospital at Pine Ridge and met the tribal representatives. The hospital equipment was old except for the laboratory, and staff morale was low. Several of the staff physicians, assigned to the Pine Ridge Hospital, were openly resentful and eager to leave.

Pine Ridge itself was small, with seventy percent unemployment and little local business except for small stores. It was a dry community, but residents drove fifty miles to Whiteclay, Nebraska, to buy liquor. This was often consumed on the return trip to Pine Ridge, with devastating results. The highway had the reputation of being the most accident prone in South Dakota. As we explored the community, we crossed a small bridge where a woman was attempting to drag home her drunk husband, a hapless situation. This was not a suitable site for medical students.

The next morning we were passengers on a small plane to fly across the state to Aberdeen. En route we tried to avoid several sets of thunderheads, unsuccessfully. We entered the center of one storm, where our plane was buffeted about with such violence that I thought we would not survive. That afternoon we flew to Balcourt, the center of the Turtle Mountain reservation for the Chippewa Indians, on the North Dakota border with Canada. The Indian Health Hospital was well staffed with two family practitioners who had been there for seven years apiece. They were proud of their accomplishments, one of which was to have a large-print circular file in the emergency room. This featured details of the treatment of major emergencies usually encountered and their treatment. The part of the file that was needed for a particular emergency was easily seen from anywhere in the room. This feature could be easily adapted to emergency rooms elsewhere and was a real advance in care instructions for the entire staff. We met a few patients, all of whom were pleased with their care. As we left, our plane took us over a small lake on the shores of which were cottages, the homes of many of the Cherokee.

We then drove to Eagle Butte, a Lakota Sioux reservation. Our assistant dean had been adopted by the Lakota and was welcomed warmly by the tribal leaders. The hospital itself appeared to be well equipped but had a serious staffing problem. The American Medical Association attempted to recruit physicians, some of whom were past retirement. Other doctors were fleeing unsatisfactory practice situations, and most were unqualified for the general type of physician needed in this situation. Most of the physicians remained only a few weeks, creating irregular staffing. The tribal council, upset about the quality of physicians supplied, was in the process of discontinuing the contract. The tribal council hoped to remedy this by taking over the medical program just as it had done previously with the dental program, which now had three full-time dentists.

With its physician program in flux, this would not be a satisfactory program for medical students, and, like Pine Ridge, needed to be excluded from the Stanford plans. The amount of alcoholism, coupled with the uncertainty of competent physician supervision, created problems that had to be solved before allowing medical students to participate.

We summarized details of our visit in a report to the faculty at Stanford. We recommended that only one of the Dakota sites be considered, the Chippewa reservation with its well-run and well-staffed hospital. The other recommended site for good teaching was the Zuni Indian Health Hospital in New Mexico.

After submitting our recommendations regarding programs for students at Zuni and Chippewa reservations, we thanked L.C. for her involvement in the visit to North and South Dakota. Several of the programs wanted her to join them, and one set of tribal leaders wanted to hire her, even though she was a second-year medical student at the time.

A few days later I was called to see a fifty-year-old man with respiratory difficulties. He lived in a first-floor apartment not far from the Valley Medical Center in San Jose and was quite short of breath, using his accessory respiratory muscles to aid his breathing. His fingertips were blue, as were his lips, and his barrel chest was accented by his efforts. These symptoms indicated a man with serious respiratory problems, probably best treated with oxygen and medication in a hospital. He refused this, saying that he could not afford hospitalization, and resisted my suggestions. I recommended some blood gas studies, which he also refused.

I told him that any more smoking would certainly kill him, and threw his bedside cigarette packet in the wastebasket. I was going to arrange nasal oxygen for him and planned to see him in two days. I placed him on medication for bronchitis, but again with the admonition: ABSOLUTELY NO SMOKING.

In two days he appeared better, and in a week he was much improved. Two weeks later, however, I learned that he was in the hospital, and believing that his respiratory problems were worse, I was surprised to find him in bed with one leg in traction. He had felt so much better that he tried to ride a bicycle, ran into a tree and broke his leg. Obviously his breathing was much better and he no longer needed the oxygen.

During the first year at Stanford, I became acquainted with many of the preceptors for students. One was Ralph Merkley, a medical school classmate who was well liked by the students. His office in Cupertino was easy to reach, and I occasionally asked him to help me with classroom teaching. Unfortunately, such efforts were not rewarded by the medical school, which I felt was unfair to the practicing physicians. Of course the full-time physicians involved in teaching were rewarded with their salaries, but there was no compensation for outlying preceptors in private practice.

Another physician who I felt offered much to students was Michael Witte, who was boarded in family medicine and pediatrics, the same credentials that gave me so much breadth in practice. He was in charge of the Point Reyes Clinic at Point Reyes Station, about fifty miles north of San Francisco. This was situated in an area of natural beauty with well-wooded hills bordered by the rocky shores of the Pacific, straddling the San Andreas fault, and the recipient of much earthquake activity. The surrounding Point Reyes National Seashore Sanctuary was a nature preserve of spectacular beauty.

The Point Reyes Clinic provided services in a thirty- to forty-mile radius, a mostly rural, multiethnic, relatively poor area, but also home to San Francisco commuters. Farm workers in the numerous dairy and cattle farms, fishermen, small farmers and park employees, retirees, and Coast Guard Station employees made up many other patients.

Michael Witte, the only physician in the clinic, had not enjoyed a vacation in over seven years, and hearing of his dilemma, I was able to be relieved from my medical school duties to substitute for him for two weeks. I wanted to take a second-year Stanford student, Jose Prieto, fluent in Spanish, to work with me. I started in the office at nine o-clock on November 2, 1984, but was so busy that there was no time for orientation from the competent staff of three nurse midwives, two nurse practitioners, one nurse, one secretary, and one medical records technician. I was overwhelmed by phone calls and so many patients to see that I wasn't able to write in charts, but the staff was most helpful and covered for my inadequacies. Late in the afternoon, one of our midwives reported that a home labor was not progressing well for a sixteen-year-old primiparous (first pregnancy) patient. We both decided that a specialist consultation was necessary at Marin County Hospital, thirty miles away. I was to meet them there as soon as possible. But at closing time of the clinic, the thirty-year-old wife of a Coast Guardsman came in with numbness and weakness of her right arm and severe pain in her right shoulder. She had been seen by an emergency ambulance team, who obtained an electrocardiogram to rule out heart disease, and referred her to our clinic for further study. After a cursory examination, I decided that she had atypical migraine without a headache. Most migraine attacks are associated with headaches, but not always. I started an appropriate medication, with a promise to see her on a house call in the early morning.

The drive to Marin County Hospital was over winding, hilly roads, a forty-minute trip. Our patient was unhappily struggling with her first labor, while her husband, equally young, tried haplessly to help. Connected to monitors, she was confined to her bed, a non-physiological arrangement for someone in early labor. As there was no progress over the next four hours, her obstetrician decided to augment her labor with pitocin and the addition of epidural analgesia. That required a scalp monitor for the baby and an intrauterine pressure catheter to complete the wiring of patient and fetus. Every aspect of the labor was being recorded—audibly and visually. At this point, the patient and her husband were obviously upset over this artificial environment for what was supposed to be a normal labor. Gradually this fear was modified as I explained to the father the function of this machinery. The obstetrician, who spoke Spanish fluently, was most accommodating with the mother and father.

By three in the morning, the baby was delivered uneventfully, a lovely baby girl. Her parents were overjoyed, and I left the midwife to stay with the family for a few hours while I returned to my simple apartment as dawn was emerging, although it was most difficult to stay awake while driving. Two hours of sleep, then up to make a house call on the patient with a migraine equivalent. I was joined by Jose Prieto, who had arrived during the night. We found the patient improved, though she continued to have weakness of her right hand.

After office hours, we received a call from one of the nurse-midwives about a patient in labor in an isolated home high in the hills. Jose and I left, became lost, but finally, after driving crazily around precipitous turns, found the home. We were greeted by six geese that loudly announced our presence. The family was happy to see the physician but not the medical student, whom I had to escort back to the clinic, where we would await a call to be present for the delivery. The call came at three AM, and again I was met by the six geese, but I had an opportunity to observe a midwife with a thousand deliveries in her experience perform with unusual skill (better than most obstetricians.)

On Sunday, one of our patients was in active labor. She was scheduled for a hospital delivery. We made a house call to ascertain her status—five to six centimeters dilated. I hoped we could make it to the hospital in time, about thirty miles away. Jose and I followed in our car; upon arrival, we found her fully dilated. Jose delivered the baby with me at his side. The baby was a lusty boy. After summarizing the details of the delivery in the hospital record, Jose and I stopped to see about progress with mother and child. We were surprised to find father, mother, and baby all in bed together watching the Sunday football game.

The next day, just as we were about to close, a lobster-red, hyperventilating, woodsman-type man appeared, seemingly in great distress. He had been stung by a yellow jacket half an hour earlier, and suddenly noted generalized itching, puffy lips, and hives. He had hopped onto his motorcycle and sped to our clinic. We gave him a large injection of epinephrine, then Benadryl, and started an intravenous, followed by a call to the paramedics. His poor response to our treatment dictated the need for a transfer to Marin General Hospital.

"I can't go, Doc, I have no money."

"You have to go; you need more treatment, and the clinic is closed in five minutes."

"The hospital will ruin me. . . . I have hardly enough to pay for gas for my motorcycle."

What to do? Reluctantly, Jose and I decided to let him stay in the clinic for further treatment. We continued with intermittent adrenalin and intravenous cortisone-like medications such as prednisone for the next three and a half hours beyond closing time. We found a tiny TV set so that he could watch *Monday Night Football.* When it seemed safe to discharge him, we drove him home to his wife. Where else can you find this type of personal service? Anticipating some night deliveries, we were in bed by ten, certain that the previous night's schedule would be repeated. We slept all night!

The next day, Jose was now confident enough to do prenatal checks alone. However, he also met a patient in his late sixties who maintained that he was the "world's champion rock skipper." He skipped stones across smooth water, a pastime I recalled as a child. "I can skip a rock farther than any man alive," he said, as he recounted past world championships when jugs of wine were offered to winners in their divisions. He won three divisions and three jugs of wine before being disqualified until the finals late that afternoon. He and his friends proceeded to drink up the prizes and at the time of the finals, he was thoroughly ossified, my term for intoxication. However, he rose shakily to the occasion and skipped his rock more than thirty skips, beating his closest competitor and previous record holder by six. This colorful gentleman, with other details of his past, was to return for a full history and physical exam for Jose to complete by himself, I acting only as an observer.

Follow-up about our patient with the unusual migraine showed her to be progressing adequately.

A child with asthma, upon questioning, had ingested a number of peanuts one week ago, the peanuts causing a coughing and choking episode. Because of the danger of obstruction from a foreign body (peanut), we sent the child for an X-ray. There was nothing suggesting a local obstruction of the type seen with a peanut ingestion.

The next day was our day off, Wednesday, and we met a community representative for minority affairs from the West Marin County Health Department. He told of the more than two hundred families from Mexico working on the many dairy and cattle ranches in this area, and of the paucity of services for these families. He invited us to a Head Start potluck next week, and proved to be a wonderful source of local culture and events.

After handling phone calls, during which we learned that several of our patients seen yesterday were better, we took the afternoon off. We decided to hike to some of the sights of Point Reyes National Seashore, heading to Arch Rock, about four miles from the clinic. En route with a misty rain punctuating our venture, we passed huge Douglas firs, rare in this part of California—usually seen only hundreds of miles north. When we reached the ocean, unknown to us we were standing on the arch of Arch Rock and obviously could not see it. The beach, over one hundred feet below, was too difficult to reach, so we retraced our steps, but found it an ordeal the last mile. We both appreciated our poor conditioning and took a long nap at our simple quarters.

The next day, our first patient was a seventy-year-old woman, crying, complaining that she was losing her mind and that all of her relatives had abandoned her. Sad, lonely, and depressed, she was the personification of dejection. She explained, "This is a different community; people have their own lives to live."

We wanted to share with her by inviting her to a senior-citizen lunch to be held at noon in Point Reyes Station. When we met her there, she was a different woman, lively, wanting to introduce us to other seniors. She asked: "Will you give us a little speech?" Obviously her self-esteem had been low and our presence was somewhat supportive. We planned to continue, perhaps by making a house call soon to coordinate our support with local mental health services.

In contrast, we saw many young prenatal patients, always happy, anticipatory, hopeful, even though some had a paucity of resources. By now, Jose was skillful in evaluating prenatal patients and did this alone; I came into the room only at the end of his evaluation. To watch this increasing confidence in a student is one of the pleasures of teaching. Each student is a unique person with his or her own attributes and weaknesses. The responsibility of the teacher is to find the attributes, and to capitalize on those that minimize and often overcome any weaknesses.

Students, in turn, often instruct the teacher. Already that week, Jose had suggested several important considerations and had uncovered overlooked information while taking a history, thereby strengthening the adage: "Two heads are better than one." I hoped that in addition to gaining confidence in relating to different patients, a most important skill in a developing physician, he would learn some office laboratory techniques, often poorly taught in medical school. Also, by making house calls with one of the nurse practitioners, or with me, he would appreciate the family environment in a manner not possible in the office.

Later in the day, we saw a woman who, visiting for the first time, wanted a full physical examination to ascertain her fitness for a total fast! Forty to fifty pounds too heavy, with hypertension, she was accustomed to a partial bottle of wine daily. With a recent divorce and its devastating effect on her self-esteem, she presented a challenge. As with many patients, she had a complex personality. She was a skilled artist in the past, a former runner who placed well in one of the most grueling cross-country races in the Bay Area. "I let myself go," she commented, "but now is the time to start living again." We outlined a brief program, and Jose surprised her with a telephone call a few days later with the results of her laboratory tests and offered support for her dwindling self-esteem. Depression is a common problem, and in treating such patients, the physician must always be aware of the possibility of suicide. Thus, we planned to keep supervising this woman closely.

Our next patient was a sixty-one-year-old woman, looking much older, who entered the examining room with so tiny a presence that I almost placed her in the children's room. Her weight was only eighty pounds. She was using every bit of her energy to breathe, with all of the muscles of her neck struggling to assist her intercostal muscles and diaphragm to achieve reasonable oxygenation. Even this was inadequate, as exhibited by her blue fingertips and lips. She was pleased to report, "I've just switched to Carltons because they are low in tar." Her hematocrit was fifty-five percent, well above the normal for a woman, and indicated that she was making many more red blood cells than average to allow maximum oxygen-carrying capacity—similar to that of natives living high in the Andes. "You must stop smoking NOW," I told her. We told her to use our "hot line" to help her with withdrawal symptoms. All of our staff would cooperate in this effort. She called the next morning, angry, because she was unable to talk with her friends. I gave her an appointment for the next day, at which time I placed her on a medicine that modifies withdrawal symptoms.

The fisherman who had a serious reaction to a yellow-jacket sting a few days before, returned with a recurrence of his hives. A shark fisherman who was anxious to get out in his boat again said, "Don't take too much time, Doc, the sharks are really biting." We didn't, and he did get back to his boat with little delay.

The next morning at 4:30 I was called by a patient with inability to sleep, asthma, and a fussy child, and she was beside herself. I suggested that she come in now, not realizing the time in my groggy state. Minimal treatment and much discussion of associated problems resulted in a more relaxed mother—and doctor. Now 5:30, time to sleep on a Saturday morning.

In the morning I saw a woman with a staphylococcal infection of her hand, secondary to a similar infection of her lover. I soaked her hand in hot water for a half hour, gave her a large injection of penicillin, and placed her on oral penicillin, with an appointment to see her again in two days. A few hours later her boyfriend called and I placed him on the same treatment— such are the various paths of love.

A woman brought her child for a quick check to rule out an ear infection. She seemed very suspicious of how I might harm her child during the examination, and I became inwardly offended, trying to hide my impatience with her overly protective manner. After she had left, our secretary confided that this woman's sister had killed her mother—enough to explain her strange behavior.

Our recent patient who had stopped smoking was worried that the sudden cessation would affect her heart. I reassured her that it would be especially beneficial to her heart. As I talked with her, I learned that she had been a member of the Vatican Council in Rome, and was instrumental in formulating the Vatican II statement regarding nuclear war. I realized that such hidden achievements are not disclosed during casual or hurried visits.

This leads me to a favorite topic, that of the hustle and bustle of the usual medical practice, which allows only a superficial knowledge of the patient as a person. Sometimes that unknown person is central to the success of therapy, which in most instances is more than just the pills or shots prescribed. In the patient with the smoking problem, her personality responded to the authority of the Catholic bishops with whom she worked on Vatican II. In the future, she may well respond to strong and well-considered recommendations from us.

A number of telephone calls, always important in family practice, completed the morning. After a quick lunch, I prepared to do some hiking, in the rain, this being Saturday afternoon. Of course, I always carry a pager with me, since there is no one else to cover the practice for emergencies. A new hiking path had been opened to Limatour Beach near Drake's Bay. It's a wonderful birding area with many marshes for shorebirds. I was prepared to walk a few miles along the beach, but the penetrating rain soaked my pack and was a threat to my camera. I did notice a few dead birds, covered with oil from a recently sunk tanker that had produced a huge oil slick and threatened the beaches of Point Reyes Seashore Sanctuary. During the next week there were many dead birds, a reminder that oil has mixed benefits, positive for humans, negative for sea life.

When I returned, I received a phone call from the woman with a staphylococcal infection. Now that her lover was also on treatment, could their skins touch? "Of course," I responded.

At two thirty in the morning, the pager rang. Two women in labor, one with a breech, whom the midwife has already referred to a consulting ob-gyn specialist, and the other, in Mill Valley, a home delivery one hour from the clinic. After a circuitous drive through hilly one-way streets in Mill Valley, Jose and I found the home, perched precipitously high on a mountainside. It commanded a spectacular view of the city and bay below, and was nestled among a grove of beautiful pines, such that one would not suspect nearby neighbors. The patient, now in active labor, was resting on a futon, her husband at one side and a close friend at the other. The nurse-midwife calmly examined the patient and informed her that she was progressing well, now at three centimeters dilatation. She used a battery-operated dop-tone fetoscope to monitor the baby's heart rate, checking every fifteen to twenty minutes.

The patient was encouraged to drink water or juice. She could shower or soak in the bathtub when she wished, and was encouraged to walk about when she wanted to. At one point she sat down to play a few notes on the piano!

As labor progressed, the nurse-midwife interacted more, always softly, supportive, and encouraging. Her husband and friend were pleased to have watched videotapes about birthing, and, as a result, understood expectations from them during different stages of labor. Though the mother-to-be occasionally screamed in pain, her husband and friend joked with her and massaged her frequently. The family dog slept through much of the process, but occasionally wandered over from the fireplace to wag an encouraging tail.

Sometimes the patient felt more comfortable sitting on the toilet seat, where she spent part of the time in labor; at other times she was more comfortable on knees and elbows; often she lay in a semi-sitting position on one side. I was impressed with the freedom of motion supported at home, in contrast to the restricting environment of the usual hospital labor room, where wires, tubes, intravenous solutions, and monitors are often used in such profusion that the patient has difficulty moving. Such inhibitions must slow the process of labor, an observation corroborated by the clinic midwives.

As contractions became more frequent, and the patient felt the desire to push, we all became more supportive. The midwife sat cross-legged opposite the patient's perineum, where she could assist easily. Soon the baby's head was crowning and the perineum stretched to what appeared to be impossible dimensions. As the baby's head finally "oozed" through the perineum, the midwife molded and protected it from tears or lacerations. The shoulders were deftly delivered and finally a baby girl appeared and the infant was suctioned.

Then the magic and all-important gasp! Immediately mother and dad showed the most beautiful smiles, kissed, and were close to their baby and completely oblivious to their surroundings. Since the infant had a very slow heart rate, too slow for comfort, I suctioned the nose and throat again and gave the infant a few puffs of oxygen from a portable oxygen tank at the bedside. Immediately the color and activity improved, and the baby, upon being placed on the breast, nursed vigorously, so much so that the mother said to her husband: "It's okay for her, even though so strong, but I would never let you do this." The placenta was delivered uneventfully and the umbilical cord was examined to make certain that it had the normal three vessels. The midwife performed a careful examination of the vagina, which showed only superficial lacerations, or "skid marks," as evidence of the recent birth.

Happiness, contentment, fulfillment, a sharing of creation, as mother, father, friend, and baby embraced; we left them alone in their wonderment and ecstasy. The midwife was to remain for two hours to make certain that there was no postpartum bleeding. I thanked the parents for letting us be present, and they thanked me for my cheery smile.

The smile that remained with me was for the memory of those two parents as they first realized that their new arrival was fine, was actually born and was in their image. No Madonna and Child were more beautiful. I left in the approaching dawn for an important antinuclear meeting in San Francisco, a chance to counteract the vast destructive forces that, if uncontrolled, threaten to cancel out all the creative efforts I had just witnessed—not only for man, but also for other living species, and the earthly environment that nurtures all life.

Jose was to return with the nurse-midwife so that he could pick up his car to drive home to Palo Alto for a brief respite.

I was headed for "Who Speaks for Earth?" an Armistice Day Coalition for Men at the Masonic Auditorium in San Francisco, Sunday November 11, 1984. Some of the comments:

'We know who speaks for the nations, but who speaks for the human species, who speaks for Earth?"—Carl Sagan

Rusty Schweicher, one of the astronauts: "The beauty of the earth from space is indescribable. There are no boundaries. The blue is overwhelming. In space, I had the feeling that this was truly mother earth, without which there is no way for us to survive."

The conference, which was televised simultaneously by satellite to the Soviet Union, placed my priorities on a different level. Whatever else, we must stop nuclear armament and do it soon. Time will not wait, especially when we realize that computers, not humans, may make the final decisions regarding the release of missiles. With faulty chips, errors in programming, it is possible for annihilation to occur in ten or fifteen minutes.

The first patient on the following day was a Spanish-speaking woman in a state of catatonia. This is a noncommunicative state in which patients with psychological problems retreat into themselves. She had postpartum psychosis following delivery of her fourth baby, and was on several strong drugs to control her symptoms. Very slow in her responses, she exhibited uncontrolled twitching in her right arm and leg. The husband was distraught, as were the many relatives who accompanied her. Unable to care for her three children and new baby, she was a tremendous burden to her relatives and friends, all of whom had large families and lived on isolated ranches.

In most situations, such a patient would be confined to a hospital-supervised program, but this was impossible, because as an illegal alien from Mexico she was ineligible for medical and other public services. If she sought such help, she would be immediately deported to Mexico. We decided to try to treat her at home with the cooperation of a Spanish-speaking aide. Her baby, initially weighing less than two pounds, had been hospitalized for many months. The mother was isolated more than thirty miles from the hospital. Her husband was working two jobs to support the family; thus hospital visits were rare, on weekends only.

No wonder she was seeking solace in a world not reachable by others. To further increase her inadequacy, when the infant was discharged, she was confronted with a fetal monitor, which recorded every breath of the infant twenty-four hours a day. Any irregularity was signaled by a loud alarm, galvanizing relatives to stimulate breathing in this still-premature baby. There was no chance to nurse this infant, nor to bond after many months of separation, adding to her stress, which was almost overwhelming under the circumstances.

A very busy day at the office, and I received a call at five o'clock.

"Doctor, I have asthma and I am unable to relax."

"Can you meet me at the office?" I asked.

"No, I feel too tired," she said.

"What do you have for medicines at home?" I asked. "You have all the proper medicines for your asthma, try a little more of this and I will call you in an hour." One hour later she was better.

At three in the morning she called again.

"Doctor, I can't sleep, and my baby is crying and pooping all the time." (tears) "Can you get a medicine to stop her pooping so that I can get some sleep?"

"Come right over to the office and I will check you and the baby," I offered sleepily.

I was too tired to do any driving.

"I'm too tired, and besides, it's raining," she said.

"Try it anyway. I'll have some tea for you."

Time passed, half an hour, then three-quarters of an hour; finally, I heard a car outside, and the door opened, disclosing a thoroughly distraught, whimpering, and exhausted mother with a somewhat malnourished child in her arms. I examined the mother to find that her chest was clear, and, knowing that her trip on curving roads in a driving rain was not easy, I assumed that a temporary increase in the adrenalin in her system offered a temporary relief. I gave her a small injection of epinephrine (the same as adrenalin) and a few minutes later she felt better.

"She keeps on pooping, doctor, how will I stop the poops? She just poops, poops, and poops"

"What do you feed her?"

"All kinds of vegetables, bread and cereal. Is that okay?"

"She looks a little underweight; bring her in for a complete exam later this week."

"I'm sick of poop. I've been shoveling it for two days."

"Shoveling it for two days, what do you mean?"

"Just what I said, Doc. I've been shoveling poop. I have a compost pile and I just got a load of horse manure to mix in. I'm tired of shoveling that poop." Now the reason for her recurrent attack of asthma became evident—an allergy to horses, common, and possibly triggered by shoveling horse manure.

"Thanks for the tea, Doc. I'm breathing better. You must be tired."

"Just a bit."

I was tired after two weeks of practice. How did Dr. Witte keep this up week after week? Sleep intervened for the next two to three hours; I awoke just in time for office hours.

As office hours came to a close, it was time to summarize notes in the charts, then to turn in early for some sleep.

Knock, knock again and again.

"Come in."

"Hey, man, I thought you were going to the Head Start potluck with me tonight," said a community organizer with the West Marin Health Department.

"No, I didn't forget, good to see you."

"How about joining me for a beer at the Western Saloon, we have time."

"Sure, meet you there in half an hour. I am trying to finish these records."

I headed one block away for the Western Saloon, a real cowboy bar, complete with swinging doors, an old weather-beaten sign, a long curved bar, a jukebox, and, in the back, a pool table, complete with a green-shaded lamp. The men at the bar were not armed; they didn't need to be, for they were all over six feet tall with arms like tree trunks. They were as weather-beaten as the sign outside. I had come to realize that everything in Point Reyes is weather-beaten: people, cars, bars, trees, and after five to six days of rain—even the weather! I found the community organizer at a table and joined him for a Beck's beer, imported but a favorite locally.

We walked to the Dance Palace, an all-purpose community building in the center of town and the site of the Head Start potluck party. But none of the Head Start families was there. Where were they? I was reassured that they would appear as soon as the cows were milked and the chores completed. As predicted, they appeared en masse in an hour. There were many children, appearing like a yearly production in some families. Some brought tapes of Mexican music, which enlivened the atmosphere and brought smiles to many.

The potluck surprises, favorite foods for many who attended, were sumptuous and varied. I took photos of many families, who offered to pay me for them, but I told them they would be available without charge in a week. On my ever-present harmonica, I played a few Spanish songs for the children, especially. The announcement of the schedule of the Head Start mini-bus was greeted enthusiastically, for it visited each ranch and was loaded with toys, games, and picture books for the children, all of which they would exchange upon arrival of the next bus one month later. This helped relieve the isolation of living on remote farms.

Just as the party was to close, our almost catatonic patient appeared and started eating voraciously. She even smiled as I put an arm around her and assured her in Spanish that she was getting better.

After a short walk to the clinic, where I was rooming, and when I was about to turn out the light, the community organizer appeared and wanted to stay the night. I replied: "*Mi casa es su casa*" (my house is your house) and invited him to stay.

The phone rang at ten that night. Jose Prieto was calling to say that his car was disabled in the pouring rain. He would try to limp back to Palo Alto and return when it was repaired. I had the next day off, Wednesday; thus, his tardiness was not a burden.

The next few days were busy, punctuated by two more home deliveries, a hospital admission, and follow-up calls on some of our problem patients. The man with the wasp sting was now over his reaction. The woman with the unusual migraine was fine. The baby with the poops was better and on a more compatible diet; the two smokers were over their initial withdrawal problems. By this time, I was so tired that I could not drive. Jose acted as a chauffeur, and we shared all responsibilities. His progress to a self-sufficient student, with many new skills, was exciting and satisfying to an admiring preceptor.

At the end of our last day, we visited Dr. Witte, well tanned, who had just returned with his wife from a wonderful vacation in the Caribbean. We were invited to spend the night at his home as we reported on the patients we had seen. We enjoyed a breakfast prepared by his wife, then left, tired but exhilarated by our two-week adventures. This was an education for us both. I reported to the faculty about Jose Prieto's outstanding and remarkable progress and when time permitted wrote a detailed diary of the two weeks of a practice that challenged all of my clinical skills.

When I returned to our family practice clinic in San Jose, I learned that it had become a refuge for some of the AIDS patients from San Francisco. Some felt that they were unwilling guinea pigs for varieties of new treatments in San Francisco. Our clinic director welcomed them, and word soon spread that we were a caring and understanding program. I met several of these patients, one of whom, a Mexican-American, was referred to me by the visiting nurses. He was in the late stages of his illness, but wanted to continue home care. I visited his home, to find him somewhat emaciated, in no pain, but with poor appetite and depressed. On the second visit, he voiced a desire to visit his brother in Hawaii; would we allow him to do so? After discussing it with his family and the home care nurse, we all agreed that he should go.

Arrangements were made for the visit, and accompanied by the nurse to the airport, he made the trip. Two weeks later, he returned, obviously happier after a satisfying visit with his brother. I made several other home visits and placed him on a hospice-type regimen, overseen by his nurse with a daily visit. Within two weeks of his return, he was in a terminal state, semi-comatose, unable to eat, having some pain that required medication. I was called late one night to see him, close to death, and remained for the next few hours. When he died, the family called the undertaker, who upon arrival realized that he was an AIDS patient and refused to accept his body. "If you refuse, your name will be publicized all over the San Jose papers," I threatened. "There are no risks to you as long as you wear gloves and are careful with needles." It did not take long for a decision; the undertaker cooperated. During the next two weeks, I visited the family twice to be of support in their grieving.

Another AIDS patient was a thirty-year-old man who wanted to spend his last days with his sister in Ohio. I tried to make him comfortable for the trip and after the second house call he was ready. I called his sister to make certain that his trip was uneventful, and made some suggestions for further care and hospice availability. As with the previous patient, he had many qualities that attracted me to become a concerned, non judgmental care-giver.

Peter McConarty, M.D., was a student with the Migrant Farm Worker Project at the University of Rochester many years ago. I had visited him at his clinic and was impressed with what he was trying to accomplish in the Mission District. One evening I received a phone call that he was hospitalized at San Francisco General Hospital with five bullet wounds. I hurried to the hospital, fearing the worst, and learned that a disgruntled patient had shot and killed the director of the clinic and shot Peter as he emerged from an examining room. Fortunately, all of the wounds were superficial. His wife, a nurse, was there. After talking with her later, I learned that she was so frightened about this, and about the future of her two children, that the family would probably leave the area. I felt that it was a wise decision, and heard that they were planning to move to Fitchburg, Massachusetts, where he was to become the director of a University of Massachusetts family practice teaching program. Peter and Donna were an outstanding and caring couple, and Dotty and I wished them well.

A pediatrician invited me to East Palo Alto, where he was director of a pediatric clinic. Palo Alto is a relatively well-to-do area with superb medical facilities. On the other side of an expressway is East Palo Alto. It featured a largely Mexican-American and African-American population, few viable stores (most being boarded up), and mostly substandard housing. Stanford Medical School had little interest in this area, even though there was a great need for better medical facilities. The pediatrician worked in less than adequate facilities, but occasionally had a medical student helping. Visiting nurses supplied home visiting and worked closely with him.

I was impressed with the contrast of the fine housing and stores on the Stanford side of the expressway and the poverty on the east side. Sometimes a student would indicate an interest, as did a sophomore African-American Stanford medical student, who visited with me a few times, and wanted to study a method for evaluating high blood lead levels in children by a simple method compared to a more expensive standard method. I helped sponsor him in this project, with the pediatrician giving approval.

While at Stanford, Dotty and I were active attendees at Quaker meetings in Palo Alto, where I became an antinuclear activist and a nonviolence advocate. We remained with the Friends during our Alviso and Stanford employment and continued that contact throughout the remainder of my career.

Meanwhile, Stanford had decided that the Division of Community and family Medicine was to be placed under the Department of Medicine. Our chairman, Dr. Count Gibson, was close to retirement, and had delegated some of his responsibilities to others. Since the Department of Medicine values its staff by research publications, it would not value the service aims of the family practice division as a high priority. Our division, though active with students, preceptors, training physician assistants, and working with under- served populations, had produced few scientific papers. Publications are important in recognizing academic accomplishments, not something in my favor, having published only five papers in my career.

Always interested in working with the underserved and poor, I was also distressed to find that the San Jose Family Medicine Clinic had upgraded its fees so that many of the neighborhood poor would be eliminated from the program. Where would they go for care? They would need to seek care at the Valley Medical Center, a half-hour bus trip away, known for its problem of long waiting times in an already overburdened clinic.

While exploring opportunities in medical journals, I saw an ad from Dartmouth Medical School, in New Hampshire, for a family physician, and was invited to visit. Dotty and I were well received by the faculty, which sponsored a family practice clinic and had developed a preceptor program for first- and second-year students. I did not relish the thought of leaving Stanford and the unfinished development of the Zuni and the Chippewa Indian programs, but hoped there would be sufficient interest to promote those teaching and service opportunities. We left with some misgivings, for our three children, plus two grandchildren, were in the West. Originally we were New Englanders, and would be returning to a familiar climate and other friends and family.

Dartmouth Programs

*I*n ten-degree weather we moved to Hanover, New Hampshire, and I prepared to start work on the first week of January 1986. We rented a small condominium close to the medical school and within easy commuting distance of the clinic. Some of my colleagues in the clinic were: a seasoned family physician; a family physician who had a half-time research project at the medical school; and a former dean of the medical school, an internist. We received funding from Dartmouth Medical School to help us with teaching medical students, who played an active role in each afternoon clinic.

One of my earlier patients was a man with cancer of the pancreas, who needed palliative home care and frequent house calls. His wife and two children in high school shared care giving, and I visited frequently for dual purposes: one making certain that he was comfortable and another to support his family.

Another patient was a former nurse with rheumatoid arthritis, house bound in a second-floor apartment, who required an occasional home visit. She became so interested in the medical student who accompanied me that I acted as an observer.

The visiting nurses suggested that I see an older man who lived in a cabin about ten miles from the clinic, was suspicious of doctors, never followed orders, and would not come into a doctor's office. He cut his own wood, and obtained food from a son who lived nearby. He suffered from chronic osteomyelitis from an old leg injury, but was otherwise reasonably healthy. I dressed his wound, which had been present for at least ten years, and planned to see him weekly as needed. I knew that I could not cure his osteomyelitis (a deep bone infection) and decided to share calls with a visiting nurse to change his wound dressings twice weekly.

Another patient, a former paratrooper, a heavy smoker who had worked in nearby chalk mines when he was younger, had chronic obstructive lung disease. He was a skeleton of his previous self, and developed frequent bouts of bronchitis, which I treated at home. I knew I could not affect his lifetime smoking habit and could offer only episodic care.

One of my first students was an African-American woman from New York City, who was suffering culture shock from being immersed in a mostly white community in Hanover. Her Brooklyn church had been a big support before her move to Dartmouth, but we had no African-American-oriented church in the vicinity. She seemed uncertain of herself in the clinic, and I tried to take extra teaching time with her. She accompanied me on house calls, one of which was at the home of the nurse with arthritis. The patient liked her so much that she wanted her to accompany me on future house calls, which, of course, was easily arranged. Over several months, the student developed a close relationship with this nurse, beneficial to both. Our student was characterized by a fine, caring attitude, one of her sterling attributes throughout her career.

One of our many student preceptors was a family practitioner in Putney, Vermont. He had a colorful career, one aspect of which was with Quakers during the Vietnam conflict. Following the war, the Quakers were the only Americans allowed in Hanoi, for rehabilitation work in the hospitals. He was one of those Quakers. As one of our finest teachers, he always had plenty of time for students in a well organized-practice.

Our preceptors included many who were close to the medical school and those as distant as Brattleboro, or Concord, or Woodsville, all about fifty miles away. The first-and second-year students had didactic sessions at the medical school to learn the rudiments of history taking and physical diagnosis. They visited their preceptors once a week. These sessions started during the first week of medical school and were a practical way to correlate classroom teaching to real live patients under the supervision of doctors in their offices. Students were pleased to be introduced to live patients so early in their careers, and were eager participants.

I visited each preceptor at least once during the year, and returned with suggestions from preceptors for improving our teaching at the medical school. Most students were enthusiastic about this early experience when most of their classes dealt with basic science— subjects, important, but better when woven into clinical experiences.

During these years, I moved from the Family Practice Clinic to full time at Dartmouth Medical School, continuing with the preceptors and first-and second-year students. I served on the admissions committee for the medical school for three years. Part of the admissions process was a thirty-minute interview, which I enjoyed. The faculty felt these personal interviews were helpful in understanding students and improving the selection process.

Students had various experiences, including the Peace Corps, working with the underserved in many countries, or working with the homeless or on ambulance emergency teams. Some were former nurses and nurse practitioners. Time spent with these students was most rewarding to me.

While the preceptorship program for students was prospering as of January 1, 1989, one of its preceptors of the Mt. Mooselaukee Clinic in Warren, New Hampshire, a family practice physician, had provided around-the-clock service for four years. He was popular with patients and medical students. His National Health Service funds were recalled in 1988, and with three children to support, he moved to Plymouth, New Hampshire, about twenty miles from Warren, for a partnership with another physician. Both provided partial coverage for three days a week in Warren, but were able to provide only acute, illness-oriented services.

Preventive services, such as well-child and immunization clinics, ceased, and chronic disease teaching, hypertension screening, and prenatal instruction were curtailed. Local nursing home supervision had been drastically reduced. Teaching of medical students from Dartmouth Medical School stopped. The director and the clinic board applied unsuccessfully for a Robert Wood Johnson Foundation grant to continue needed services. Because of the relative poverty of many of the patients, the program was unable to hire another physician and approached Dartmouth Medical School for help.

A partial solution to providing adequate health care for the area was evident, following a series of meetings with the community health staff at Dartmouth and members of the Mt. Mooselaukee board. A family physician from Dartmouth would be hired to work three days per week in the clinic, with emergency services supplied by Woodsville Hospital (thirty miles distant) or Plymouth Hospital (twenty miles away). Prenatal and delivery services would be supplied by nurse-midwives from Dartmouth-Hitchcock Medical Center. Dartmouth Medical students would continue at the clinic. The board would function as before.

Interested citizens from the community would be taught health concepts, and be available as "community health facilitators." They would circulate from the clinic to schools, homes, and nursing homes to monitor health needs throughout the community. They would meet once weekly at the clinic to evaluate progress and engage in further teaching.

The only physician available from Dartmouth was myself, and after an introductory meeting with the staff and board for approval, I was accepted, and started immediately. Though the clinic was forty miles from my home, I was able to reach it in forty-five minutes if traffic allowed. This was an opportunity for me: a rural clinic with great needs, and methods to meet those needs. The close personal relationship with patients was much to my liking.

Hours from nine to five allowed time for house calls before and after hours. The plan to have medical students was also to my liking, for they provided questions and stimuli to better clinical practices. I formulated ideal scenarios, plans that I presented to the faculty at Dartmouth:

1. A training program for our community health facilitators or workers.

2. Maintain close contacts with the Dartmouth-Hitchcock Midwifery program to conduct weekly Women's Health Clinics and Prenatal Clinics, and to provide obstetrical needs at Dartmouth-Hitchcock Medical Center.

3. Weekly staff conferences to incorporate positive input from each member.

4. Attract consultants with a variety of skills.

5. Establish frequent contact with Dartmouth-Hitchcock Medical Center and Plymouth and Woodsville Hospitals for referrals.

6. Visit, as time permits, all Mt. Mooselaukee Health Center patients when hospitalized. This is important for relationships with patients, even though some will not be under my care.

7. Maintain close contact with the visiting nurses in the area to assist in the care of some of our homebound patients.

Shortly after I started practice, this appeared in one of the local newspapers:

Local Doctor Recertified as Family Practice Specialist
Dr. John F. Radebaugh, M.D. of Warren, has been recertified as a diplomate of the American Board of Family Practice, as a result of passing a recertification examination by the board. He thus maintains a specialist status in the medical specialty of family practice. The Academy is the first specialty to require members to take continuing study and a recertification examination every seven years.

Such publicity never hurts when trying to restablish a rural health clinic. Several potential consultants offered their services, including the chief surgeon at Alice Peck Day Hospital in Lebanon, New Hampshire; a Lebanon family practitioner with whom I had practiced; and a former rheumatologist.

I soon learned that this practice would challenge all of my previous skills, and more. One of my first patients was a man with serious hypertensive and cardiovascular problems who, though friendly enough, did not follow directions, according to the nurse. I adjusted his medications, and wanted to see him weekly until his pressure was controlled. He did follow directions, but still proved a challenge.

Another was a sixty-year-old woman with transposition of the great vessels, a condition that requires extensive cardiac surgery in infancy. That was not available in her youth. Somehow she survived and was now under the skillful management of one of the Dartmouth-Hitchcock cardiologists. Her too frequent visits to Hitchcock caused her to seek our help. I agreed, with the supervision of her cardiologist, and would even make house calls when necessary.

Another, seen for the first time on a house call, was a thirty-five-year-old woman with severe multiple sclerosis, which was keeping her bedridden. I learned that she was only one of four multiple sclerosis patients in Warren, quite unusual in a small community.

Others included children from broken families, often with no transportation and very limited resources. We had no van and relied on the visiting nurses to bring in these patients for clinic appointments, though I often made house calls in follow up.

In contrast, we had some patients, usually retired, who could afford all of our services. One was a woman with rheumatoid arthritis, a former Boston museum director who needed to be seen at home, a delightful woman who had retired to Warren.

Another challenging patient was a man with traumatic quadriplegia (paralysis from the neck down, involving all four limbs), who was understandably bitter about his condition. He drove a specially equipped vehicle, and often needed treatment for recurrent kidney infections. He always asked to see me, but almost always on house calls. On house calls I occasionally asked to see all of a patient's medicines. Frequently, I noted medicines stored for many years, often outdated for usefulness, as with this patient. Simplifying was easy to accomplish, and usually appreciated.

The students were a big help, and were able to examine patients in an adjacent room, where I could easily supervise. They often accompanied me on house calls, which offer superb teaching environments. They were also excellent teachers for the community health workers during their weekly teaching sessions.

My three-year-stint at Mt. Mooselaukee Health Center was one of the most satisfying of my long career, for here I could establish a close relationship with many patients, and was able to make a number of house calls. It was evident to me that this could be a valuable way to involve students. As a result, I established a protocol that I presented to the Community and Family Medicine faculty: Plain Doctoring, or House Calls with John. From the protocol: "The education of a medical student, or even a college or high school student contemplating a career in medicine, should include the milieu of the patient being studied.

"To do this the student needs to make home visits. In this setting, the student is in the familiar surroundings of the patient, or on the patient's turf. Other members of the family may be present, pets, siblings, status of repairs of the home, placed a framework around the center of attention, the patient.

"An appreciation of the family, to which a student can easily relate, creates a common bond between the student and the patient one in which the student or physician is on equal ground. This eliminates the artificial barriers of the white coat, the office or clinic, and, of course, the hospital— all of which are threatening to the patient. These barriers interfere with true teaching, much of which comes from the patient. Home teaching has been shown to have an even more lasting effect upon the student than classroom or textbook learning."—John Radebaugh M.D.

This is a copy of a letter to the dean about "Plain Doctoring, or House Calls with John" by one of our students. She was a Peace Corps volunteer in the Tonga Islands in past years.

Dear Dean McCollum:

I am writing to you to share my enthusiasm for a one-day elective I recently attended. The informal elective is the work of Dr. John Radebaugh, whom you know as a faculty member in the Department of Community and Family Medicine. For some time now, Dr. Radebaugh has been exploring the idea of a single day elective for medical students which might be called "Plain Doctoring" or "House Calls with John." The elective consists of a full day of visiting four or more families, several visits with health care professionals in the community, and several readings in epidemiology and family medicine.

May 30 was my day to spend with Dr. Radebaugh, a country doctor, professor and friend. Our day began in Bowler Auditorium for Pediatric Grand Rounds. Radiology was our next stop. The two of us reviewed films with the Radiology staff for patients we would see later that day. We then proceeded to the depths of the hospital to the autopsy suite where a pathology resident presented his gross specimens and his findings for a recently deceased patient. Not unexpectedly, the partially fixed brain tissue revealed a peach-sized necrotic mass characteristic of glioblastoma multiforme (a highly malignant brain tumor). We were later to visit this patient's family in their home in Warren, N.H.

Dr. Radebaugh and I, with a long list of patients names and addresses, packed ourselves into his car. Our first stop was New England Industries in Lebanon, N.H., which produces machine parts. Dr. Radebaugh had met previously with the owner of the company, who this day welcomed us and presented us with ear plugs and safety glasses. We had come to see Mr. R.M., a patient of Dr. Radebaugh's who has persistent problems with nasal polyps.

Weaving through the maze of giant metal monsters, noisily pounding frail strips of steel into a precise geometry, we found R.M. rolling a drum of industrial chemicals into the plant's back door. R. M. told me that his nasal polyps had been treated surgically several times, but continued to reappear, and caused him difficulty breathing.

The etiology of the recurrent polyps was unclear. Mr. R.M. felt that the chemicals that he was working with here at the plant contributed to the development of the polyps. R.M. gave us a tour of the plant. We examined the labeling on many of the drums of chemicals that he was frequently exposed to. Mr. R.M. asked me to climb the stairs leading to the operator's station in a machine which chemically and mechanically washed some of the metals used in production. He turned on the machine so I could experience the sharp odor and harsh racket of his daily working conditions. This was a new experience for this Dartmouth Medical student from suburban Concord, Massachusetts.

We proceeded on to the home of Mr. and Mrs. D.C., a middle-aged, middle-class couple. They were expecting us and we sat and chatted about his recent hospitalization for COPD (chronic obstructive pulmonary disease). We examined his lungs and heart, and we gave him a report on the chest films we had reviewed earlier in the day in radiology.

Our next stop was Mr. R., a frail but good-humored ninety-two-year-old New Hampshire farmer whose wife died ten years ago, leaving him to live alone with his horse team, advanced bilateral cataracts, osteomyelitis and severe hearing loss. As we approached his tiny run-down wooden shack nestled in the woods just off the dirt road, I asked myself how it could be that I have had a full four years of medical school here at Dartmouth, yet have been so successfully sheltered from New Hampshire's poverty.

My country doctor and I lunched for fifty cents at the Lebanon Senior Citizens' Center. There I met many octa, septa, and perhaps even non-agenarians, most of whom knew Dr. Radebaugh well and had many sores, aches or pains to report, along with jokes and some bits of gossip. It was valuable for me, now a new M.D., to get a sense of the services available in the community. I met a social worker and a community health worker and now I feel I have a better sense of what can be available for the elderly in the Lebanon area.

From here we headed towards Warren, N.H., stopping to meet a nurse who directs the Visiting Nurse Association in Canaan. I had a chance to hear her opinions about community health care in the Upper Valley and to share my views. Dr. Radebaugh caught up on the news about patients he was following.

We visited, counseled and examined seven more patients during the remainder of the afternoon, including a very elegant woman painter in her scrupulously cared for colonial, and an overweight hypertensive in his cat-infested trailer home. One highlight of the afternoon was meeting and examining a delightful middle-aged woman with transposition of the great vessels.

I could go on with tales of these individuals, their medical histories, their homes, their jokes, but the day was long and as Dean of Dartmouth Medical School, I realize that your time for reading student letters is short. I write only to share my memories and to offer a vote of support for what, I hope, will at some time be developed into a formal elective which will offer this opportunity to other medical students. I feel grateful to have attended a medical school which encourages a broad perspective in medicine and supports enthusiastic faculty as Dr. John Radebaugh.

I have enclosed my address in New Mexico as I will be starting out as an intern just one week from today! Please keep in touch. Call if you are in the Albuquerque area and let me know as well of any future trips you may take to the Tonga Islands.

Sincerely,

Patricia Ruze

The Community Health Workers for the Mt. Mooselaukee Health Center met once weekly for teaching and reporting on their experiences, and over the time that I was a member of the center, it provided valuable help. We invited a clinical psychologist whom I knew well to conduct a teaching session. She had been a recipient of the New York Society of Clinical Psychologists Holocaust Memorial Award for 1982 in recognition of her achievements in counseling relatives of victims of the Holocaust. Her efforts for justice, freedom, and equality, both in the cause of racial freedom in the South during the sixties and as a leader among psychologists devoted to action as well as to theory and words, were exceptional!

During her visit, she addressed the problem of physical and sexual abuse and asked the workers whether any had experienced such abuses. Reluctantly, many for the first time discussed their painful memories. Two-thirds of the women related such episodes in their childhoods. She mentioned that these episodes often had long-lasting effects, which could be ameliorated by open discussion with others, much as was happening during this teaching session.

As a physician, I became dependent on their judgment regarding victims of abuse, or of violence in the home. In some cases, opinions of a community worker were crucial in understanding such problems. Two of the male board members were helpful to me in different ways.

One Monday morning I met a patient, head of the local Alcoholics Anonymous program, who came to the office profoundly drunk. He had been sober for twenty years, but started drinking steadily during the previous three days. I could sedate him, and advise him, but knew that my advice was not going to be successful. One of the community workers was active with AA, and I called to have him see the patient in the office, which he did. I wanted him to be an advocate, one who would be available for support and counseling during the next few weeks, while I would see the patient in the office to provide professional help.

Two days later the patient was improved, and four days later he appeared to be over the episode. During the ensuing year he was completely dry, probably due to the concerted efforts of our board member. He still continues as the AA leader in the community.

Another male community worker offered his nearby home, if I ever needed to stay overnight due to weather or emergencies. This was most reassuring, for the winter snowstorms were sometimes severe enough to preclude my driving home. I took his kind offer on several occasions.

On April 13–15, 1993, Cesar Chavez, the United Farm Workers Union leader, visited the medical school, invited by L.B., a second-year student and the daughter of farm laborers. Cesar Chavez spoke to a packed auditorium at Webster Hall. The title of his talk was "Non-Violence and Social Change."

John with patient, Dartmouth clinic (1986)

"I don't think any one event, or any one day, or any one action, or any one confrontation wins or loses a battle. You keep that in mind and be practical about it. It's foolish then to try and gamble everything on one roll of the dice—which is what violence gets down to. I think the practical person has a better chance of dealing with non-violence than people who are dreamers or impractical. We are not non-violent because we want to save our souls. We're non-violent because we want to get some social justice for our workers.

"If all you are interested in is going around being non-violent and so concerned about saving yourself, at some point the whole thing breaks down and you say to yourself, 'Well, let them be violent as long as I'm non-violent' or you begin to think that it's okay to lose the battle as long as you remain non-violent. The idea is that you have to win and be non-violent. That's extremely important. You've got to be non-violent and you've got to win with non-violence."

He continued: "Pesticides are poison and workers are often exposed to these pesticides." He illustrated with a video of *No Grapes,* a documentary produced by the United Farm Workers Union. This film depicted the consequences of pesticides on farm workers in California and the south-

John with ever-present harmonica (1986)

western states. In the film, children of farm workers exposed to pesticides are shown with birth defects.

"Pesticides are believed to cause many forms of cancer, as well as sterility, skin disease, and respiratory problems. For example, some towns in California have cancer rates for four- to twelve-year-olds that exceed national averages by 800 percent. Pesticides are known to contaminate water supplies of local communities near grape fields," Chavez said.

He finished to a standing ovation of many minutes' duration, followed by other meetings in which students had an opportunity to interact with him—his strongest attribute.

Though very busy with meetings and teaching in one of the classes, he was allowed time to prepare for an upcoming trial in Arizona, a lawsuit by the owner of the same land that Chavez's father had to give up in the Depression. At that time, the Chavez family joined the migrant stream, and young Cesar attended thirty-seven schools before he completed the seventh grade. This grower was suing the United Farm Workers Union, and the trial was scheduled for a few days after Cesar's return to the West Coast. Rooming at the Aquinas House, a Catholic Center for the college, he had an opportunity for a much needed rest and to prepare to testify.

His son-in-law, who was being groomed to be president of the union upon the retirement of Cesar, accompanied him. I drove them to Logan Airport in Boston, where we were delayed by a traffic jam of some duration.

```
┌─────────────────────────────────────────────────────────────┐
│  ◤◥ UNITED FARM WORKERS of AMERICA AFL-CIO                   │
│        National Headquarters: La Paz, Keene, California 93570 │
│                      (805) 822-5571                          │
│                                                               │
│                                                               │
│  April 21, 1993                                               │
│                                                               │
│  Dr. John Radebaugh                                           │
│  Dartmouth Medical School                                     │
│  Office of Minority Affairs                                   │
│  Hanover, N.H. 03755-3833                                     │
│                                                               │
│  Dear John,                                                   │
│                                                               │
│  Thank you very much for enabling me to make a presentation   │
│  at Dartmouth last week. The entire visit was a success and   │
│  both Arturo and I feel very good about it. I also enjoyed    │
│  the time we got to spend together while we were driving.     │
│                                                               │
│  It is good news to discover that after volunteering in the   │
│  past, you are still very interested in continuing to         │
│  actively support us. I know that you and Lorraine put a      │
│  lot of effort into preparing for our visit and it clearly    │
│  showed during the two days we were there. I am also very     │
│  glad to know that a Support Committee is being organized in  │
│  the area to continue to work on promoting the grape boycott. │
│                                                               │
│  Thank you very much for your long standing support John. I   │
│  appreciate all the work you have done and will continue to   │
│  do on behalf of the United Farm Workers.                     │
│                                                               │
│  Sincerely,                                                   │
│                                                               │
│  [signature]                                                  │
│                                                               │
│  Cesar E. Chavez, President                                   │
│  United farm Workers of America                               │
└─────────────────────────────────────────────────────────────┘
```

I pulled out my ever-present harmonica and played a few union songs, much to the surprise of Cesar, who exclaimed: "How do you play that thing?"

"It's real easy, you could learn in a very short time," I replied.

In the many years I have known Cesar Chavez, this was the longest time I had ever spent with him. It was a real privilege for me, for I was always in awe of him. I received a fine letter from him, written only a few days after his return to union headquarters.

On the 23rd of April, he died suddenly, probably of a heart attack. His funeral was attended by thirty-thousand people, including political leaders, farm workers, and Catholic and Protestant clergy, with resulting eulogies from many parts of the country. Despite overwhelming odds, he led thousands of farm workers to decent working and living conditions. He attracted many admirers, certainly including Dotty and me. Our years with him represent the outstanding and most meaningful times for both of us.

My purpose in working at the Mt. Mooselaukee Health Center was to be an interim physician until a permanent physician was available. A retired cardiologist, who lived about twenty miles away, had accepted the position. Under the director, the staff, patients, and community enjoyed a barbecue to celebrate the changing of physicians. A surprise participant was a patient whom I had seen on many house calls because of her inability to visit the clinic—yet, she did appear, and for the first time was quite talkative. Another surprise was the woman with transposition of the great vessels, accompanied by her daughter; a farmer with severe diabetes, who rarely visited the clinic, and was seen only on house calls, also attended. Board members were all present and joined the director in their comments. I left with a warm feeling and comments that I would like to return occasionally with students to do a few teaching house calls—with permission, of course.

Shortly after my retirement, in July 1991, I took part in the development of the Good Neighbor Health Center in White River Junction, Vermont. With a paid manager, and a donated building from a neighboring church, this volunteer program was open three nights per week. We accepted patients from throughout the two-state area, regardless of ability to pay. One of our first patients drove 120 miles to have a physical exam and for the doctor to sign an approval for his truck driver's license—he had been refused such services locally because of his inability to pay.

Another was a single parent with two children, from Virginia. She was homeless, unable to find shelter in many communities along the Atlantic Coast, and finally ended in a desperate condition in White River Junction. She visited the clinic with her children for medical problems. We referred her to The Haven next door, a temporary shelter for the homeless. She lived there for two months; the children went to the local school, and she enrolled in a secretarial program . Finally, she found a job in Bellows Falls, Vermont. Several years later she returned with a contribution for The Haven. She was independent and the children were doing well in school.

During one of our early clinics, a woman and her baby were brought to the clinic by police. She was lost in White River Junction, and had been abandoned by her husband in a rural area. Somehow she was able to gather enough money for bus fare to White River Junction. After treating her sick child, we referred her next door to The Haven, where a room was available, and social services helped her find a small apartment in town.

A family who had lost medical insurance when the breadwinner lost his job visited from fifty miles away for medical care. Always able to be independent in the past, they were unable to afford private medical care, and returned several times for other illnesses.

Among visitors to the Good Neighbor Health Center were two Athabaskan natives. They were interested in our program because it had many similarities to their own in western Alaska. There were no roads in their area, and they provided primary care isolated from outside help except by short-wave radio and bush-plane services. They accompanied me on a house call to a woman with chronic low back pain and some arthritic symptoms in other parts of her body. She was lonely, and discouraged with her progress under my care, and I was pleased to see them relate warmly to the patient. They tried some traditional methods of massage, along with encouragement, and after two hours the patient felt better. I returned with them in twenty-four hours, and the patient, now much better, wanted them to continue their treatment.

For a number of years we communicated with the two Alaskans by mail, new friends with respect for each other's skills and willing to learn more. They wanted me to visit them, if ever possible, and I replied that I would try. I told them that a nephew married an Athabaskan woman who came from the same part of Alaska, and they replied that they knew the family. I never was able to afford to visit them in Alaska.

Subsequent events with the Good Neighbor Health Center included the supervision by the local visiting nurse service, which required its physicians to carry malpractice insurance, thus excluding me from participation for financial reasons.

At this time, the program hired a new director, who had extensive experience with similar clinics in other parts of the country and overseas. Under her supervision, the Good Neighbor Health Clinic received enough funds through contributions to occupy a vacant public library, which was converted into a fine clinic with adequate room for three dentists and more medical exam rooms. Many physicians volunteered from the Dartmouth-Hitchcock Medical Center, which also accepted referrals at reduced costs from the clinic. The expanded clinic was busy from the start, and the caring staff provided service with dignity to anyone who sought its services.

Next door, The Haven, which for years turned away more families per year than it was able to accept, doubled its size under a new director. It was able to take in eight new families, and to increase its teaching and social service offerings significantly. It was the only homeless program north of New York able to offer around-the-clock lodging and schooling.

One Thanksgiving Day, I happened to drive by The Haven and noticed a woman knocking at the entrance door, with a child waiting in a battered car. "The clothing and food stores are closed today," I told her. "Is there any way I can help?"

"Yes," she replied. "We have no food, and I was hoping to find some here."

I thought of the unhappy and poorly nourished child in the car. "Follow me; I think I know where we can find some food."

I took her to a surplus clothing program in Lebanon across the river, with the hope that it would have some suggestions. It was cold outside. The woman and her daughter picked out some items, but there was no food. Across the street was the largest Catholic church in the area, but the priest told us the church had delivered all of its Thanksgiving baskets earlier that day.

What to do, for they both looked forlorn and hungry. I had twenty-five dollars in my wallet, which I gave to her. I wrote down her name and suggested that she return to The Haven the next morning for more substantial food assistance (usually a week's supply of food). I went home with a warm feeling, realizing that this was only a modicum of the help this woman really needed. The next morning I called The Haven. I asked them to look for her and to offer other aid, including social services.

I often ate lunch at the Bugbee Senior Center in White River Junction, where the social worker, realizing that some people were no longer able to come to the center, wanted to set up a visiting program for them. A few of us, after a three-week training program, were assigned a former Bugbee senior for a home visiting program. We were to report our experiences once weekly at the Bugbee Center. My assigned person was N.C., who lived alone in a small rural cottage. She had metastatic breast cancer of eighteen years' duration. When the primary was found in one breast, she underwent a partial mastectomy and bilateral removal of the ovaries. She was subjected to chemo and X-ray therapy under the close supervision of one of the Dartmouth-Hitchcock oncologists and a radiologist.

N.C. suggested that we document her "journey of discovery" visits in a small diary. She proved to be easy to visit, and had a wide range of experiences and observations. During this house call, I reassured her that I did not want to intrude, and would have her review everything that I recorded for approval. As we talked, she reminisced about growing up in Brooklyn, New York, her support for humanitarian and social causes, and her respect for trade unions and their importance in upholding human rights. Despite the recurrent pain in her shoulder and back, she felt reasonably well and very talkative.

"In 1976," she said, "I was diagnosed with cancer and moved to East Thetford, where my husband died of cancer ten years ago. At that time I did much soul-searching, trying to consider a career in art, my main skill." I looked at her scenery paintings on the walls of her home and admired her talent. "Dr. M. has been a learning experience for me, as he has been treating me for eighteen and a half years since my cancer was first diagnosed." Later, I met her oncologist, and appreciated his attention to the many complications due to her original tumor.

A few visits later, she had to be transferred to a nursing home for more intensive treatment for recurrent pain.

"I know that I am going to die."

"I feel so alone."

"I wish I could kill myself, but I wouldn't do it myself."

Amid her tears, I promised to return tomorrow. The next day, I asked, "Are you suffering?"

"What a question. No one has ever asked me that. When I am having pain, it is a simple request. Here the staff goes by the books and is slow to treat the pain. It is very hard to wait because it becomes worse if they don't treat it promptly. One of the things that helped me at home was that I was able to control things myself. Here they give me my meds, but sometimes only if I remind them. No one explains to me what pill is for what; they just give them to me without any explanation."

Three months later she was still in the nursing home and was concerned whether Medicare would be able to help her enough if she were at home. "If I am going to accept Medicare money to be given to the visiting nurses," she said, "they would hire someone during the weekdays only. Now I learn that I can have someone on weekends also. I wanted to have a friend interview people initially, but then she went on vacation. I wish that I had some input into the person who will be caring for me. Suppose I don't like her."

Constantly aware of her limited resources at the end of her life, she commented: "I have decided to prepay my funeral expenses, and called the same funeral home that took care of my husband." Prices were quoted to her and seemed beyond her present resources. "I think that the whole funeral industry is corrupt and takes advantage of the families of the dead. If I prepay, it will cut my savings to less than two thousand dollars, making me eligible for Medicaid coverage." She showed me her copy of the potential funeral bill, which would have taken most of her savings, a shock to her and to me.

A few days later, while visiting her, I learned that she was not entitled to any further radiation therapy because it was not covered by Medicare. It would cover only a few doctor visits per year to the nursing home, a revelation to me. "I don't know why I cry so frequently, almost always when I am alone," she told me. "Maybe it is because of my anger at being here. Without my husband, one son is the only relative on whom I can rely."

Finally she was discharged to her home, where she said, "I don't want to be alone when I die," as she remembered several of her neighbors at the nursing home, dying with no one in attendance. She recalled the death of her husband, who was able to sit on the porch of their modest home and appreciate the ambience and gentle wind.

I had introduced her to F.P., a Ph.D. psychologist, who was living at a retirement community in Hanover. I became acquainted with her while I was a board member for that program, and befriended her, because as a Jewish New Yorker, she had few friends among other residents. She was a warm and skilled therapist, who, just as N.C. did, wanted to be useful. The two women were instant friends, both from New York City, both Jewish, and both interested in social problems.

Conversation moved to the feelings of older people, and F.P. mentioned her dislike of euphemisms such as "golden years" and "senior citizens." "What are everyone else, junior citizens?" she asked. The women talked about their lack of mobility, their dependency on others for transportation, shopping, or events they wished to attend. F.P. harkened back to the civil rights movement under Martin Luther King Jr. in the South. She was in Mississippi when several of her companion civil rights workers were killed. Activists had to be careful regarding their behavior because of their associations with both black and white companions. The police were always a threat. Both women were in tears at this point.

Two months later, F.P. developed acute abdominal pain at her retirement community, where I saw her and expressed concern about her condition, which was felt to be due to constipation. This continued all weekend. When I expressed concern to the nursing staff, they informed me that they knew her well and that I was not her doctor. I called one day later, to find her in the hospital emergency room, where her surgeon diagnosed a perforated bowel with peritonitis, and her condition was too precarious even to operate. Realizing the hopelessness of her situation, she tried to say, "Good-bye, I will never see you again." I tried to counter with the thought that she was too much of a fighter to succumb to this illness, but she knew better. A half hour later she died, two hours before the arrival of her daughters from New York City. To communicate this to N.C. was devastating, for she wanted every detail of the illness and to know the results of the autopsy, which showed a perforated duodenal ulcer with secondary peritonitis—but also, a surprise to everyone, the early brain findings of Alzheimer's disease. The loss of F.P. was deeply felt by N.C., her daughters, and me. She was a talented, courageous woman.

During the next few weeks, N.C. suffered a series of fractures, all with little trauma, and related to weakening from metastases to her bones. These were splinted rather than casted, and she was placed on increased opiates for pain. Fortunately, she was improved by Thanksgiving Day and allowed to be reunited with her two sons, in her own home.

A few days later she fell on a slippery floor in her bathroom, fractured her femur, and had to be admitted at Dartmouth-Hitchcock Medical Center. As a blizzard outside cut my visit short, I produced the ever-present harmonica and played, "'Tis a Gift to Be Simple," one of her favorite melodies.

A nurse who had known N.C. for eighteen years visited her during each hospital admission, and did so at this time. This nurse, with her understanding and caring, was very supportive. Another close friend and neighbor, a devout Baptist, visited N.C. at least three or four times weekly. N.C., though Jewish, considered attending the neighbor's Baptist church in East Thetford, but was too sick to do so. On my next visit there was a definite change in her demeanor, a seeming resignation to the inevitable for the first time. Each day there was a definite weakening, to eating almost nothing, drinking little, and being semi-stuporous. She was transferred to Alice Peck Day Hospital, with the finest rehabilitation unit in the area, for her terminal care. Occasionally, I played two of her favorite songs on the harmonica, "How Great Thou Art" and "Amazing Grace," sometimes seeing a faint smile in response.

I telephoned her older son, who arrived from Massachusetts in two hours, and he wanted to be at her bedside for a few hours. About one hour later she died, and he later told me that he was glad to be there, for it was an hour that could never be repeated. She died on Christmas Eve and five days later, at her memorial service, her older son participated. He gave a moving eulogy. Surviving nineteen years of metastatic breast cancer, she maintained her dignity and love of beauty till the very end. She was a woman who inspired all who knew her with her courage, her love for others, and her optimism even in the face of overwhelming odds. Her diary, "Journey of Discovery," was a beautiful memorial and a tribute to her physician, friends, and care givers. It also was a tribute to F.P., the social worker who visited her a number of times during her last months. The two shared experiences, emotions, which both of them cherished in their autumn of life. As a humble student, I learned much from these two unusual and talented women.

The Bugbee Senior Center had another impressive visitor, Frances Davies, a ninety-year-old African-American musician, who was active at the center. She started her career as a classical pianist in New York and hired an agent at the age of eighteen. He heard her sing and persuaded her to take voice lessons. Her first job was lead singer with Cab Calloway, which catapulted her to a traveling career with other orchestra leaders. She was Bess in *Porgy and Bess*, and eventually the director of a USO show in the Pacific theater in World War II. Married to a man who became her manager, she continued with her music on her return to the United States. After the death of her husband, she added her organizing skills to developing an acting troupe.

When she retired, she moved to White River Junction to be near a friend, whom she affectionately called her niece. She directed the Bugbee Troupers, a singing group, which attracted a number of older folk, including me, to join her weekly rehearsals. She arranged monthly performances in senior centers, nursing homes, and retirement communities in the White River, Lebanon, and Hanover areas. Occasionally she was hospitalized for short illnesses and eventually had to move to a nursing home. But she never gave up her music at the Bugbee Center, and found transportation to her beloved Troupers.

As she became less ambulatory, I visited her frequently at the nursing home, where she directed musical programs. She returned to the Bugbee Center when her condition permitted. During this time she was intellectually alert and competent, in contrast to her problems with ambulation, and I began working with her in much the same manner as with N.C. and F.P. Eventually she died of pneumonia, at age ninety-three, and I felt honored to be asked to give one of the eulogies at a large memorial service attended by all of the Bugbee staff, nursing home staff, and many friends. She was a most unusual and gregarious woman, with talents that mobilized many in the Bugbee Center to be more active. She had many admirers.

A few months later I received a phone call from a former medical school classmate. As a member of the board of the East Corinth, Vermont, health clinic, she wanted me to visit, and to help recruit a temporary physician. The present family practitioner was unable to pay her medical school loans and support her family of two children on her small salary at that clinic. She was planning to leave to join a larger and better-paying program in New York

State, but had developed a devoted following at the East Corinth clinic. She would be difficult to replace.

After several visits, and meeting the staff and board members, and realizing how difficult it is to recruit physicians for such a clinic, I volunteered to work there on an interim basis. It was a much easier commute than to the previous clinic in New Hampshire, but needed a five-day week from me. Nighttime and weekend coverage was available from a family practice clinic ten miles away. As in the past, I approached the clinic with ideas, most acceptable, others impractical, and totally supported the previous physician's caring philosophy. Fortunately, I could share some of the responsibilities with a physician's assistant (similar to a nurse practitioner), a fine nurse and a cordial receptionist.

Shortly after I arrived, I received another phone call from the second-year Dartmouth medical student who invited and helped host Cesar Chavez a few months previously. Active in minority affairs, she wondered whether I would see a freshman who was a quadriplegic, the first ever at Dartmouth Medical School, and offer some encouragement He was quite disheartened about his grades and whether he could remain in school. Originally from Korea, at the age of eighteen, while practicing with the U.S. gymnastics team in Colorado, he attempted a flip that had never been perfected. He fractured a neck vertebra, with resulting quadriplegia. He underwent a long rehabilitation program before attending college. Though he had been accepted at Dartmouth Medical School two years earlier, he had to delay entrance until many architectural barriers, but not all, were corrected.

After a long conversation, during which I realized that more than casual contact was necessary, I offered him a chance to work with me a few days a week at the East Corinth Clinic. Though rural, it would be of interest in spite of his urban background. He accepted, and we began seeing patients together. Older than most medical students, he was understanding with people with chronic or depressive illnesses, and could relate easily to a variety of patients. Since he could not be separated from his wheelchair, he had to adapt his examinations to his handicap, and soon became adept at handling equipment—for example, asking a patient to roll from side to side while he listened with his stethoscope.

The staff liked him, for he was seven to ten years older than most medical students. Some patients were impressed enough to make return appointments when he was scheduled to be in the clinic. Within a month, I was able to see improvement in his outlook, and confidence in his abilities with patients.

We usually had lunch at the general store, which supplied sandwiches and soft drinks as we sat among several local residents who were regular customers. One was living in a wheelchair because of a stroke; he and S.B., our student, became quite friendly. One day this friend, who lived across the street from the general store, invited us to feed his fish in a pond behind his barn, and loaded a bucket on S.B.'s lap. The bucket was highly odorous, and later S.B. confided that he felt quite sick with the emanating smells in his lap. We fed some of the largest trout either of us had ever seen, and accepted an invitation to return to try fishing in the future. Unfortunately, we were never able to take him up on his offer, a regret to this day.

We were able to make a few house calls, one to a box-maker who lived not too far from the clinic and had severe rheumatoid arthritis. Over the ensuing months, he wanted us both to return. Another was to an older woman who was not receptive until I played a few old-time songs on my ever-present harmonica. I have always been impressed that such a simple musical instrument can erase barriers. Soon, S.B. had established himself enough that patients wanted to see him, especially if they had emotional problems. For these patients, he was especially empathic, perhaps because he had overcome so many problems himself.

Patients with bipolar disorder (manic-depressives) are often difficult to manage in an outpatient setting. The wife of one such patient visited the clinic with tales of woe, of his frequent sleeplessness when he would work all night on a project and continue this for three or four days at a stretch. He spent money without accounting for it, and at other times was quiet, almost noncommunicative, coupling this with excessive drinking. His wife mentioned that he would not come to the clinic for treatment, but did welcome the offer of my visiting with a house call. Upon arrival, I was surprised to realize that I already knew this man, for he had a catering service that often sponsored programs at Dartmouth College, where he was usually a gracious host. We agreed he would come in for an appointment, and I mentioned that I would like him to see our medical student for an interview, initially, while I consulted with a psychiatrist friend about appropriate treatment. S.B. and the patient were in tune, so to speak, and the student obtained a fine history of a condition that had been untreated for years. We started him with daily doses of lithium, a preferred drug for treatment, but that had to be monitored carefully to make certain that he was not overdosed. As with many other patients with this illness, he occasionally refused to take the medicine, with disastrous results in his behavior. He was very intelligent, so I could persuade him eventually to return to medication. Relapses were expected, but less frequent during the next few years.

Occasionally a patient would request a house call over the telephone, and I, in my ignorance of the distances in this rural area, agreed. One such patient lived about fifteen miles from the clinic. Finding her home after much difficulty, I was able to treat her for an asthmatic attack. I did not volunteer, at that distance, in the future.

Another was a ninety-nine-year-old woman with problems with infections of her feet. She had no transportation, lived alone, hauled wood for her woodstove, and was quite self-sufficient. One snowy evening, after office hours, I made a house call, dressed her infected foot, then, much to her surprise, shoveled her walk and brought in enough wood for the next couple of days. This is one of the benefits of a rural practice!

Our physician's assistant was a fine feature in the clinic, and being a woman, she was often preferred by female patients. We would have an informal meeting when I first arrived in the day to discuss patients, but saw most of our patients individually in the clinic. We would consult freely about patients, for she was bright and well read, and had considerable experience over the past ten years. She, with my encouragement, began making house calls, enhancing her usefulness to the community.

One patient arrived in a drunken stupor in his pickup truck. I offered to drive him home after his appointment and was in the process of moving my car to the waiting room exit when I spotted his truck already on the highway. Not about to chase him, I returned to the clinic. Later, I learned that he returned home safely.

Our student performed well at the clinic, though I was his preceptor for only part of a term. I did keep in touch with him at Dartmouth, and made a number of house calls at his apartment. It is not easy for a disabled student to undergo the rigors of medical school. Weather problems in winter and a propensity for bladder or skin infections often plagued him. His first two years of medical school were an ordeal for him, but he survived and did very well during his third and fourth years, which were mostly in clinics and the hospital wards.

He wanted others to be aware of the problems of disabled students, and with my help developed a hands-on wheelchair experience, during which students spent two hours following him in wheelchairs through various floors of the hospital. They appreciated the tight sleeping quarters for residents and students when on night duty, problems trying to find references on the high bookshelves of the medical library, balancing food trays while in the cafeteria, and trying to propel their chairs up slight inclines outdoors, among other challenges. Most of the students gained from this short teaching effort. S.B. initiated and performed a valuable service not available to students in most medical schools.

He went on to an internship at Cambridge City Hospital in Massachusetts, then a rehabilitation residency at Johns Hopkins Hospital, in Baltimore. He is an inspiring example of what can be accomplished in spite of a disability, with courage and persistence.

The East Corinth Clinic was a fine experience for me. I worked there for two years before a permanent physician could be located. The board, the staff, and the wonderful cross-section of patients remain a pleasant memory.

Although officially retired from Dartmouth Medical School, I enjoyed being a family practitioner, and visited Dr. Peter McConarty's Family Practice Residency Training Program in Fitchburg, Massachusetts. I knew him first as a student at University of Rochester School of Medicine and later when he was a staff member at San Francisco General Hospital. He developed a popular training program for family practitioners at Fitchburg Hospital. I was interested and wanted to join him for two days twice monthly. I found the teaching an excellent challenge to keep up with residents in training, realizing that some of them were more current than I in the latest trends in medicine.

Occasionally, I was asked to cover for a staff member who was ill, and I recall one house call vividly. A woman in her seventies, originally from Finland, needed a home visit. When I arrived, she answered the door with surprise and suspicion. "I don't know you and will not allow you to examine me," she said firmly.

"I'm not replacing your doctor, only trying to help him," I replied.

Just as she was about to close the door in my face, I reached into my bag, pulled out my still ever-present harmonica, and started playing *Finlandia*, the Finnish national anthem. There were tears in her eyes as she opened the door to welcome me in.

It was a most cordial visit, and it concluded with a request: "Please play *Finlandia* again the next time you come." I did.

Dotty and John Radebaugh (ca. 2000)

Afterthoughts

Wholehearted involvement with patients, their families, and the community provided a deep understanding of their needs as illustrated with an ancient Chinese proverb:

"I hear and I forget."

"I see and I remember."

"I do and I understand."

Relationships with patients are a two-way street, for in caring and concern for the patient, the physician, in return, receives the satisfaction of having served with dignity. Patients were great teachers, and I gained great respect for them as individuals. I learned to avoid being judgmental, enhanced by my seeing many of them in their homes.

I appreciated the overwhelming difficulties of many African-American patients facing the ingrained prejudices of the greater white community, openly expressed in the South, more subtle in the North. In either case, it was always devastating. This prejudice imprisoned the victims and the perpetrators, a blight that needs to be confronted with love—love thy neighbor as thyself. Of course similar problems confront Mexican-Americans, Puerto Ricans, and other minorities of a variety of ethnic origins, languages, and religious backgrounds.

I saw firsthand the enormous burden carried by refugees, who arrived in this country from a different culture, religion, and with perhaps different family attitudes. The self-sacrificing efforts of friends and family on behalf of new refugees were inspiring to witness. I visited and I understood, more than I could have seen in the office alone.

I respected the efforts of the United Farm Workers for equal rights, dignity in the fields, health needs, retirement benefits, fair wages for their tireless work, and their wholehearted support of their leader, Cesar Chavez. His commanding presence, characteristic of a great man, inspired workers and many volunteers, who realized that, collectively, union members could achieve much more than workers or advocates alone could ever accomplish.

In the years since Dotty and I were both volunteers, the awful realities of the present status of the union is too evident. At present there are only twenty thousand union members, a fraction of those in 1976. The shift from a liberal California political scene to one more conservative heralded the loss of collective bargaining rights. The rapid increase of immigrants from Mexico created an overabundance of workers, most of whom could be hired by growers in large numbers through the old "crew boss" system.

Though insulated by distance from field workers, we were always interested, and were especially pleased to have Cesar Chavez visit Dartmouth College, only ten days before his death on April 23, 1993. There were thirty thousand people at his funeral, attesting to his influence among farm workers and their supporters and his incredible charisma. One curtain closed on the efforts by and for farm workers and a new chapter takes over.

In summary, I will always be grateful for the influence of these individuals:

Rev. John B. Lewis, a Congregational minister and my grandfather, who was a living example of "Love thy neighbor as thyself."

Naomi Chamberlain, assistant professor of Community and Family Medicine, University of Rochester School of Medicine, who by her sensitivity to the plight of migrant farm workers reshaped my career.

Robert Haggerty, M.D., chairman of the Department of Pediatrics, University of Rochester School of Medicine, for supporting me and the Migrant Health Program through some difficult times.

Cesar Chavez, leader of the United Farm Workers of America, for his inspirational leadership through even more difficult times.

Dotty Radebaugh, who weathered many trials, and remained a constant support as we shared our lives. She exemplified the maxim I have tried to follow: "Always choose the path with heart."

David E. Lounsbury, M.D., FACP, colonel, Medical Corps, Walter Reed Army Medical Center, and an editor for Armed Services Publications, for his detailed review and criticism of the entire manuscript.

Peter Bien, Ph.D., emeritus professor of English, Dartmouth College, who reviewed the manuscript for grammatical errors.

Richard A. Aronson, M.D., M.P.H., medical director, Maternal and Child Health, Department of Health and Human Services, Augusta, Maine.

The expertise of Doug Calhoun, who solved many computer problems.

Friends meetings, where I was inspired by many members who shared their lives of service and compassion.

These experiences in many parts of the country are varied in locales, but have in common the belief that caring for patients involves love, concern, and flexibility to adapt to new situations. It includes house calls when necessary and utilizing the full complement of community services available for optimum patient care. When possible, the abilities and concerns of students add another dimension of patient care. Some of those patients and students continue to maintain a correspondence, heartening to me, an unexpected return for many years of "Plain Doctoring, or House Calls with John."

Readers' Comments

John Radebaugh is the epitome of the heart and art of medicine. As this recounting of his career makes clear, he not only practiced with those values ever in mind, but he was always looking for ways to reinforce them in his colleagues and pass them on to the next generation of care givers. His career path stretched from Maine to California; his patients varied from migrant farm workers to Ivy League professors, but his commitment to caring never wavered at any step of the way.

—*Dana Cook Grossman, Director of Publications, Dartmouth Medical School*

John Radebaugh's book is awesome, courageous, inspiring, visionary and told with wonderful humor and wit! Throughout the narrative, he put into words exactly the ideals that inspired me and others to enter the profession of medicine—the compassion, the curiosity, the advocacy for patients, the outreach and partnering with them and, ultimately, the quest for social justice that is at the heart of the medical profession—or at least, should be.

—*Richard A. Aronson, MD, Medical Director, Maternal and Child Health, Maine Dept. of Health and Human Services*

House Calls with John is a book with compelling appeal for a wide range of readers. The author's students in the Departments of Pediatrics, Preventive and Community Medicine were introduced to society's most vulnerable and neglected populations— seasonal farm workers and poverty stricken families. His insightful personality inspired workers and students to consider socially responsible careers.

—*Naomi H. Chamberlain, M.S., Assistant Professor, University of Rochester School of Medicine, and the Ship Hope*

House Calls with John is well written and contains numerous real house call experiences in a variety of venues across the country. He has had several careers of medical practice and recounts them in a pleasant, easily readable style which should resonate in the minds of many, including physicians and students, of the value of house calls.

—*Herbert K. Seymour, Falmouth, Maine*

It is encouraging to read how one person had such an impact in many under served areas of our country. A few years ago, Dartmouth Medical School named its community service award in his honor, recognizing the impact made on the world by his testifying about the needs of the migrant workers and others. It is important to know that there are still individuals who have committed their lives to those who might not otherwise receive care or be heard.

—*Sarah D. Krug, Royal Oak, Michigan*

About the Author

Dr. John Radebaugh's peripatetic career originated at Bates College, Lewiston, Maine, where he had a fine background in humanities and science. He followed at Harvard Medical School, where Dr. William Castle, a Nobel Prize winner, was one of his favorite teachers. Following a rotating internship at Mary Hitchcock Hospital in Hanover, New Hampshire, he completed training in Pediatrics at Massachusetts General Hospital in Boston.

Later he joined the pediatric faculty at University of Rochester School of Medicine. He was introduced to the terrible conditions of farm workers, and was so shocked that he helped create volunteer health clinics for these workers, which later developed into comprehensive community projects for two rural towns.

Cesar Chavez recruited him, with his wife, to volunteer with the United Farm Workers Union in the San Joaquin Valley in California. Having visited India to learn about Mahatma Gandhi's non-violent methods, Chavez applied them effectively to secure rights for farm workers. Dr. Radebaugh admired him as an outstanding leader, but exhaustion forcced him to leave after three years of service.

Returning to Harvard Medical School for additional training, Dr. Radebaugh passed boards for family medicine, and received an appointment in family community medicine at Stanford Medical School. Six years later, he was appointed to Dartmouth Medical School as a clinical associate professor of Community and Family Medicine, and continued until the time of his retirement in 1991.

In 1991, an award was established in his honor, the John F. Radebaugh Community Service Award for a deserving Dartmouth medical student in each graduating class.

In 1999, he was inducted into the Farm Worker Advocate Hall of Fame by Rural Opportunities, Inc., Rochester, New York, for many years of service to improve living and working conditions for migrant farm workers. Cesar Chavez received the same award a number of years previously.

John and his wife Dotty, who played a strong supportive role throughout his career, are retired and living in Maine.